FUNDING
YOUR
BUSINESS

FUNDING
YOUR
BUSINESS

Kenneth Winckles

**KOGAN
PAGE**

First published in Great Britain in 1988 by Kogan Page Limited, 120
Pentonville Road, London N1 9JN

British Library Cataloguing in Publication Data
Winckles, Kenneth
    Funding your business.
    1. Business enterprises — Great Britain —
    Finance
    I. Title
    338.6'041'0941   HG4135

    ISBN 1-85091-598-9

Printed and bound in Great Britain by
Billing & Sons Ltd, Worcester

Contents

Introduction

Understanding what makes a business tick inevitably requires some knowledge of the principles of finance and the meaning of the figures which portray the business in real terms, yet many managers have not acquired such an understanding and do not appreciate the meaning of the figures which regularly pass across their desks. This is a shortcoming which becomes more significant with each level of seniority and with the increasing complexity of an expanding business.

It is not good enough to leave an understanding of the figures to the 'finance man', and to rely upon him to explain the significance of what is happening. It is essential that the competent manager takes whatever steps are necessary to acquire this knowledge and understanding. Numbers are neutral. They are also international. And they have to be mastered.

Most directors have in mind the benefits attaching to a public quotation. With wider appreciation of the value of share ownership, together with government encouragement of new business formation, the opportunities now unfolding for managers, through buy-out arrangements, to acquire an interest in the business in which they have been employed, are a growing feature of the UK financial scene.

This book seeks to establish first, the manner in which the financial needs of a business should be approached, and then considers the diverse methods and sources of satisfying them. It is addressed particularly to the directors and general managers of smaller to medium-sized companies, rather than the specialist, but it is hoped that finance directors and accountants will also find it of value.

The subject matter is complex. Every chapter could be developed into a book on its own if the issues addressed were dealt with in full detail. But such in-depth treatment would be incompatible with the aims of this book, which are to assist a broad understanding of the principal considerations from the point of view of the general manager. In practice, in almost every case, relevant professional advice will be taken by the wise manager.

Lastly, it is worth making the point that reference to the application of the Companies Act 1985 relates to normal trading companies. Special rules may apply to certain banking, insurance and shipping companies.

Chapter 1
Focus on Figures

Introduction

When considering his financial requirements, the businessman will have in mind three fundamental questions:

- How much do I need, when and for what purpose?
- Where can I get it?
- What will it cost?

The answers to these simple questions are not straightforward. They involve in-depth knowledge of the business and its forward plans.

Management, markets and money

The basic steps are, first to establish the financial needs of the business within a medium-term horizon of three to five years; to determine the most appropriate type or types of finance to satisfy those needs; to explore the nature and source of finance which are available and most appropriate, and to identify those factors most likely to lead to successful funding.

Three principal elements are essential to the successful prosecution of any business:

- board of directors (management)
- markets
- money

It could be argued that there are only two because good management will identify whether or not there is a market which can be profitably serviced. And if there is not, it will seek a satisfactory alternative or abandon the project. These elements are present in every business, large or small, international or domestic, corporate or individual.

If they have to be put in order of priority, pride of place must always go to management. Money is the oil of business. It is not the business itself, unless, of course, the business is money. In either case, money cannot work or be made to work without management. Quality of management is the pre-eminent requirement of successful business – or any other successful activity for that matter. It follows, therefore, that consideration of the funding sources cannot be addressed without paying some attention to the management issues which are of direct relevance to them.

The third ingredient, markets, is also of critical importance. Successful business cannot be conducted unless there is a market which will buy the products or services of the company on a continuous basis and will yield satisfactory profits to maintain an ongoing business. If this is not the case, there cannot be a long-term business proposition. It follows, therefore, that those who are putting money at risk to finance a business will first assure themselves that satisfactory management and markets do co-exist.

Markets

So far as markets are concerned, it is not proposed to explore in detail the many issues that impinge on the existence of markets and a company's ability to serve them profitably. The business plan, to which reference is made in Chapter 2, indicates some of the factors which must be addressed by management to demonstrate its marketing capability. This is of fundamental importance to the financier who is to arrange finance for the company: he will take whatever steps he deems appropriate to satisfy himself that such markets do exist and that the company has the technical, marketing and human resources to implement its strategies with a high probability of success.

The principal concerns of the financier – and indeed the proposer – insofar as they relate to markets, will include:

- The extent to which the chosen target markets have been identified, quantified and characterised, and the methods which have been used to arrive at that analysis.
- The extent to which the markets are dynamic, and the estimated rate of change.
- The perceived benefits attaching to each of the company products and how they match the identified market. The extent to which the products have unique characteristics and how long such an advantage is likely to last.
- The perceived strengths and weaknesses of the company, and how

it proposes to reinforce strength and protect weakness.

- What marketing opportunities are likely to present themselves in the medium term.
- The nature of the competition on: their products, their perceived benefits and their financial strengths. How these compare with the proposer's products and resources.
- The capability of the organisation to analyse the markets, plan market entry and activity, and translate perceived market needs into product specifications and products.
- The financial implications, including pricing policies, product costs, margins and contributions.
- The customer support and post-sales service requirements, and the plans to provide them.
- An understanding of, and plans and methods to achieve, quality assurance in all products and services.
- The technical and design capability to develop new, attractive, cost-effective products; to innovate and adapt to changing requirements.

In view of the widespread concern among industrialists and government that the UK is failing to match the R and D efforts of its principal international competitors, it may be expected that financiers will pay more attention to this critical factor for the longer-term survival of the companies in which they invest.

This is a fundamental issue demanding the attention of every board concerned with manufacturing products.

The board of directors

The essential function of the directors is to manage the company. They are appointed, and can only be removed, by the shareholders. Apart from certain powers reserved to the shareholders by the Articles of the company or by statute, the directors acting as a board have all the powers necessary to conduct the company's business, and responsibility for doing so. The Companies Act 1985 specifies penalties for malpractice or neglect by a director, whether or not he is formally appointed. Penalties also arise from other legislation, for example the Insolvency Act 1986. The general thrust of successive Acts of Parliament has been to broaden the duties and responsibilities of directors, and to require ever more public disclosure.

Although not a trustee in law, a director in some respects has a quasi-trustee status. His primary duty is the well-being of the company. He has a wide range of responsibilities, particularly for creditors, employees

13

and shareholders. The Articles of Association establish the directors' powers and are therefore of great importance in company business. Because of the directors' central role, the board and its composition are important to all who contemplate dealings with the company. The financier's confidence in the board and management of a company is essential. The younger the company, the greater the risk to the financier: what has been achieved in preceding years is relevant to the probability of future success.

In a start-up the risk is at its greatest, with new products and an untested management. For these reasons, the competence of the board and the management will be the subject of critical review. That competence will be assessed in the light of the many impressions formed through historical association, or in the course of discussions concerning the proposal to be financed. The financier has to decide whether the proposal is soundly based and whether the board seems likely to achieve its targets. The following factors are particularly significant:

- The historical record over at least three, preferably five, years.
- The soundness and regularity of the management information.
- The methods by which case flow will be controlled.
- The thoroughness with which the business plan has been prepared and the financier's assessment of its credibility.
- The impression given as to whether the company is capable of adapting to change, indeed of managing it.

So far as the board is concerned, there are certain points which the financier will be considering:

- Is there an overall balance of skill and experience?
- The qualities, characteristics and relationship of the chairman and managing director (and whether these two positions are separately filled).
- Whether there is a competent, independent presence through at least two non-executive directors.
- The availability of competent financial advice.

The financier will be interested in the organisational structure of the company and the qualities of the senior line and functional managers, in the age and experience of these key players, their ability to work as a team, and their attitudes to the achievement of objectives.

While this in-depth interest is likely to be most evident in the case of a public offering, it will be shared by all who intend to invest in the company.

Types and sources of finance

There are only two types of finance available to a business: monies attributable to the owners of the business and those attributable to third parties, the creditors. They are fundamentally different.

Within these two broad categories of finance there are many varieties. Amounts falling due for payment within 12 months are part of the company's working capital and should therefore be related to current assets which comprise the source from which the short-term liabilities will be paid. Borrowings will be considered in detail in Chapter 3 and share capital in Chapter 4.

There are many sources of finance from which a business can obtain funds. Indeed, such is the choice available, that it is usually necessary to seek professional advice to ensure the correct choice is made without wasting valuable time.

The clearing bank will be the appropriate source of finance to satisfy the needs of many borrowers who are seeking straightforward loans. The correct nature of borrowing – whether overdraft facility, short-, medium- or long-term loan – will depend on the purpose for which the loan is required and the structure of the balance sheet.

However, the choice becomes more complicated when new capital is required or it is appropriate to structure the financing with, for example, loan conversion options.

The following list shows the main sources which may have to be considered:

- clearing banks;
- merchant banks (including similar financial services from specialist arms of the clearing banks);
- foreign banks operating in the UK;
- stockbrokers (either for public offering, private placements or client funding);
- money brokers (intermediaries, not principals);
- specialist financial brokers (factors, lessors, hire purchase);
- specialists in venture capital (UK and US);
- life funds and pension funds (many of which allocate a proportion of their assets to direct investment);
- savings banks;
- investment trusts;

It really is necessary to get the targeting right. Even given the correct 'sector' selection and a limited number of particular financial houses, considerable effort will be involved in the presentation of the proposal and in the detailed discussions which will almost certainly follow.

Be prepared for disappointments and setbacks. When financing is difficult, for start-ups or development, for instance, the process is likely to be far more demanding than many businessmen understand, negotiated against the background of stress necessarily associated with preparing for a new business or significant development in an existing business. Raising the money is only the end of the beginning.

Understanding the financial position

Whether the financier is considering lending or investing, or both, there are certain basic financial statements which are relevant to a proper understanding of the financial position of a company. They are:

- the balance sheet
- the profit and loss account
- cash flows
- financial forecasts, which embrace each of the prior categories.

Each of these will be considered in more detail. First, however, there must be an understanding of the principles applied in the preparation of financial statements.

Accounting concepts

True and fair view

The overriding consideration when preparing accounts is the presentation of a true and fair view both of the state of affairs as shown in the balance sheet and of the profit and loss account. Although Schedule 4 to the 1985 Companies Act sets out in detail the formats to be adopted in the preparation of the accounts, departure would be permissible and required if, for some reason, such presentation, when viewed as a whole, failed to portray a true and fair view. In such an event, there would be a reference to the facts in the notes to the accounts.

In this context, 'materiality' is of particular relevance. It is neither possible nor desirable to attempt a definition of 'material' which can be applied as a formula: an item is material if knowledge of it would be likely to influence the user of the financial or other statements under consideration, in the context of all the statements under consideration, and in the context of all the relevant business circumstances.

Accounting principles

The four guiding principles which apply to the preparation of any accounting statements are:

1. Going concern
   It is presumed that the company is, and will remain in the foreseeable future, a going concern. If not, a completely different view would have to be taken of many items included in the accounts which would be significantly affected by the termination of trading.

2. Consistency
   The application of consistent principles provides the best opportunity to compare items of a like nature within each accounting period, and from one period to the next. Therefore, if an accounting policy is changed, this must be noted, the reason for it given, and every effort made to provide reasonable information as to the financial consequences of the change.

3. Prudence
   This means that a conservative approach shall be adopted by not taking credit for unrealised profits and providing for all expected losses. There must be reasonable certainty in recognising profits taken into account.

4. Matching
   Accounts shall reflect all income and charges relating to the period covered, with the intention that income and related expenditures are properly matched. The incidence of cash receipts and payments is not, therefore, generally relevant in this context.

The notes that have to be attached to all accounts must be read carefully. They contain statements defining the policies adopted by a company in relation to its accounting practices. It is helpful to the reader if attention is drawn to any changes which have taken place since the last set of accounts. Many other important matters concerning the financial situation are covered in the notes.

The balance sheet

The balance sheet shows a summary of the assets and liabilities of the company as at the date the statement is prepared. The amounts included are arrived at by reference to the amounts shown in the books of the company and to the accounting policies applied to them. The balance sheet does not attempt to portray a valuation of the company and it would be quite misleading to assume that it does. Because a balance sheet portrays a position at a given time, as with a snapshot, it is most unlikely that it will be the same the day before or the day after. Indeed, there can be, and often is, significant change.

Most companies 'manage' their financial affairs to portray as favourable a view as possible of the financial structure at the year end. The notes should be examined for contingency items which may be potentially material but cannot properly be recognised in the accounts at the date of the balance sheet; for example, because it is believed the event will not occur or is too remote for assessment. They should also be carefully examined in relation to 'off-balance-sheet' financing.

Particular attention must be drawn to the use of the historical cost convention in the preparation of accounts. This is the usual treatment and means that an amount is shown in relation to its original cost, regardless of subsequent changes in the value of money. However, revaluation may be made in appropriate circumstances and, if such treatment is applied, it will be described and identified.

It will be appreciated that adopting historical cost as the basis of accounts means that the consequences of monetary devaluation (inflation) are not recognised. This is generally well understood, but it remains a fact that accounts prepared by this convention may well be inaccurate and misleading. In spite of years of consideration and debate, a generally accepted, alternative accounting basis has not emerged, although guidelines for the use of an alternative 'current cost' basis do exist.

Inflation affects both the balance sheet and the profit and loss account. It can mean that the profits shown by the accounts are illusory and that dividend distributions based on them are illegally paid, partly or wholly from capital.

Structure of the balance sheet

The balance sheet comprises three principal elements:

- assets
- liabilities
- shareholders' interests.

Total assets will always equal total liabilities plus the shareholders' funds. Therefore, total assets less liabilities will equal the shareholders' funds. This may otherwise be known as the 'net worth' of the company. The funding of the assets has therefore been provided from two totally different sources: the liabilities are amounts owed to third parties, ie creditors or borrowings. The shareholders' funds show the amount attributable to the owners of the business. The relationship and composition of these two different sources are important and will be discussed in more detail.

Assets

The Companies Act 1985 requires that assets shall be classified into three general categories:

- intangible assets
- tangible assets
- investments.

Intangible assets

Intangible assets relate mainly to development costs, to patents, licences, trade marks, etc and to goodwill. Because they are intangible it does not mean that they have no value. Indeed, they may have very high value, although difficult to quantify. The treatment and amortisation of intangibles may have a material impact on a company's financial position: the accounting policies must therefore disclose what treatment has been applied.

Goodwill presents special difficulties. Goodwill may only be included in the balance sheet if it arises from transactions which involve the giving of valuable consideration. This 'purchased' goodwill represents the difference in amount between the fair value of the consideration given and the fair value of the separable net assets acquired. It may emerge on consolidation of group accounts as the difference between the cost of acquiring a subsidiary company and the underlying net assets. The accounting standard recommended practice is not permanently to retain goodwill in the balance sheet, but normally to write it off immediately against reserves, otherwise it must be amortised through the profit and loss account on a systematic basis over its estimated useful economic life. Again, the accounting policies will disclose the basis adopted. The fact remains that goodwill may be a real business factor in the continuity of trading and, in the case of a service business based essentially on people, it will be most usual for a substantial goodwill item to emerge as a result of acquisition.

Tangible assets

As the name implies, tangible assets can be readily recognised for what they are. Broadly there are two types: 'fixed' and 'current'.

Fixed assets. Fixed assets are those by the use of which the business may be carried on. Examples are buildings, plant and machinery, vehicles etc. By their nature, they are necessary to the conduct of the business but are not intended for trading purposes. There is therefore normally no advantage in attempting to value them from one year to another. But because fixed assets are held for use by the business on a continuous basis, it is necessary to make provision for their assumed reduced economic life through the passage of time, usage and obsolescence by making charges for depreciation, or amortisation, depending on the nature of the asset. On the historical cost convention, therefore, the asset will be shown in the balance sheet at cost, less provision for depreciation (the basis for which will be described in the notes to the accounts).

There can be occasions which justify a revaluation of the fixed assets and, if so, given the overriding requirement to show a 'true and fair view', revaluation should extend to all of the fixed assets. Should a surplus over book value emerge, that amount will be carried to the 'revaluation reserve'. The reason and basis for the revaluation will require explanation in the notes to the accounts.

Current assets

By the Companies Act's definition, if an asset is not a fixed asset it must be a current asset. A current asset may be defined as one used in the course of trading, and must be classified into one of four categories:

- stocks
- debtors
- investments (marketable, ie other than those classified as fixed assets)
- cash at bank and in hand.

It may otherwise be known as 'working or circulating capital' because of the continuous process of purchase of raw materials and stocks through sales into debts and then by collection back into cash.

A current asset is in essence totally different from the fixed asset classification and must be valued at its net realisable value provided this is not greater than cost. Adequate provisions must therefore be made against any current assets which, for whatever reason, are not fully convertible into cash.

Against these assets it is correct to set off current liabilities incurred in the purchase of materials and supplies used for trading, known as *trade creditors*, other short-term creditors and provisions for expenses which have been incurred to the date of the balance sheet but not paid for.

It is the net investment in current assets less current creditors that is significant to a reading of the balance sheet, and identifies the amount of working capital employed in the business.

Investments

The third category of fixed investment relates to the holding of long-term investments. A trading company's fixed investments will comprise investments in subsidiary companies or in associated companies, and they will need to be distinguished in the balance sheet. A subsidiary company is one which is controlled by the parent company, usually by the holding of more than 50 per cent of the voting ordinary share capital of the company. In that case, the company will be required to produce consolidated accounts for the group as a whole as if it were a single entity, thus replacing the investment with the underlying assets and liabilities of the subsidiary. It must be understood, however, that this is a notional statement and does not obviate the need for the preparation of legal accounts for the parent company, emphasising that legal rights and obligations attach to each individual company rather than to the group as a whole.

Investments which do not give control, but amount to not less than 20 per cent of the target company combined with the right to exercise significant policy influence by the investor, are known as associated company investments. Accounting standards require that such are identified in the accounts: the accounting treatment is to recognise the appropriate share of the associated company profits (or losses) in the income account of the investor and to uplift the cost of the investment in the balance sheet to the extent that profits have been earned subsequent to acquisition but have not been distributed by the associate to its shareholders.

If the investment is less than 20 per cent ownership it is a trade investment, and no special accounting treatment is called for. The investment will be carried at cost, and dividends received brought into the income account at their gross value (with an appropriate charge in the taxation account).

Liabilities

The Companies Act 1985 defines the categories into which the creditors of the company shall be classified. They are set out in detail on page 156. There is a clear distinction between creditors falling due for payment within 12 months, and those payable after that period. The former will be classified in the balance sheet as an offset against the current assets, in order to disclose clearly the ability of the company to discharge its short-term creditors as they fall due in the normal course of business. Those falling due after 12 months will be shown separately.

There is a requirement to disclose in the notes to the balance sheet the following additional information:

- The aggregate amount of debts, other than those payable by instalments, which are due at least five years after the balance sheet date, together with the terms of payment and the interest rate.
- The aggregate amount of debts payable by instalments, any of which fall due at least five years after the balance sheet date and the aggregate amount of those instalments, together with the terms of payment and interest rates.

There must also be disclosed the aggregate amount of any debts in respect of which security has been given and details of the relevant security.

It should be mentioned that potential liabilities may occur subsequent to the date of the balance sheet but relate to conditions which existed at that date. Any such 'post balance sheet events' must be disclosed.

Shareholders' interests
The interests of the shareholders comprise the called-up share capital of the company, together with reserves. Some of these are of a capital nature and are therefore not generally available for distribution to shareholders except in accordance with the provisions of the Companies Act 1985. Or they may represent accumulated retained profits, which are available for distribution to shareholders.

Shareholders' interests must be classified within the following categories:

- called-up share capital, disclosing the different categories into which it is divided. Chapter 4 deals with this in more detail.
- share premium account, representing the difference between the price at which a company issues its shares and their nominal or par value.
- revaluation reserve, representing the surplus arising on the revaluation of company assets, as compared with their value in the books.
- other reserves. These comprise several different categories, such as (a) capital redemption reserve, (b) reserve for own shares (c) reserves provided by the Articles of Association and (d) other reserves.
- profit and loss account. This represents the cumulative amount of profit retained in the business. It may alternatively be known as 'the revenue reserve'.

Typical balance sheet

Balance Sheet at . . . . 19 . .

	Notes	19..	19.. (previous year)
		£	£
FIXED ASSETS			
Intangible assets			
Tangible assets			
Investments		_____	_____
		_____	_____
CURRENT ASSETS			
Stocks			
Debtors			
Investments			
Cash at bank and in hand		_____	_____
CREDITORS: amounts due within one year	(_____)	(_____)
NET CURRENT ASSETS (LIABILITIES)		_____	_____
TOTAL ASSETS LESS CURRENT LIABILITIES			
CREDITORS: amounts due after one year	( )	( )
PROVISIONS FOR LIABILITIES AND CHARGES	(_____)	(_____)
NET ASSETS (LIABILITIES)		======	======
CAPITAL AND RESERVES			
Called-up share capital			
Share premium account			
Revaluation reserve			
Other reserves			
Profit and loss account		_____	_____
TOTAL SHAREHOLDER'S FUNDS		======	======

. . . .
. . . . Directors

The accounts of a company must identify all the movements in reserves, of whatever nature.

As already explained, the total of these interests, or shareholders' funds, will equate with the net assets of the company, ie assets less liabilities.

Appendix 1 sets out the detailed contents of a balance sheet based on Format 1 included in schedule 4 to the 1985 Companies Act. The reference to 'notes' will identify by number the relevant note attached to the accounts. It will describe in greater detail how each item is made up.

Reading the balance sheet

Having taken this brief look at the structure and format of the balance sheet, it is possible to consider what inferences may be drawn about the financial position of a company. Before doing so, however, it would be as well to restate the limitations arising from the adoption of the historic cost convention and to remember that the assets shown in the balance sheet are most unlikely to coincide with the market value and certainly not any forced sale value. Nevertheless, for the purposes of a going concern the balance sheet does have very real meaning, and the previous year's comparative figures are of great help in interpreting trends.

The following points are worth noting:

- The net assets of the company are the equivalent of capital and reserves. To the share capital which has been subscribed will be added accumulated retained profits, reserves representing any surplus arising from revalued assets in excess of their cost and share premiums arising from the excess of the monies raised from new shares issued at a price in excess of the nominal value of those shares. Together these represent the capital employed in the business. It is also fairly usual to work out the net tangible assets by eliminating the intangibles from the assets. Bankers in particular will frequently apply this more stringent test for the purposes of making loans and calculating their risks.
- The ratio of borrowings in relation to capital and reserves. Judgement and prudence must be exercised by the board to hold the relative proportions on a sound basis, having regard to the nature of the company's business. It will normally be regarded as imprudent if the ratio is greater than 1:1. On the other hand, a company with no borrowings would be regarded as excessively prudent.

  In general, the cost of borrowing should be cheaper than the cost of capital. Too much prudence, therefore, will tend to depress the earnings attributable to shareholders' capital.

- The investment in net current assets is a critical element. If this is in fact a negative amount, ie current creditors exceed current assets, there is a serious difficulty. The figures are saying that the company cannot meet its short-term creditors from its short-term liquid assets. This would require some rapid action to avoid a financial crisis. The level of working capital is a constant challenge.

  Two other key relationships are revealed by the working capital. The first is frequently known as the acid test: its purpose is to relate cash, near cash and accounts receivable to current liabilities. If covered, this establishes a strong liquidity position and the ability to meet current liabilities without resorting to realising inventory.

  The second is the direct relationship of current assets to current liabilities. It is the basic test of the company's ability to meet current obligations as they fall due.

  The importance of the working capital position cannot be overemphasised. It is in this area where most financial difficulties arise, either because trading is expanding so fast that the stocks and debtors cannot be financed from internal resources or because there is laxity in the control of amounts invested in stocks and debtors or insufficient control over the payment of creditors.

- The effectiveness of debt collection by relating the amount of trade debtors to turnover. This is frequently found to be between 45 and 60 days. Again it is a cause of substantial capital employment.

- The litmus test for measuring overall management performance is the ratio of earnings to capital employed. The challenge, therefore, is to keep the net asset level under tight control and to seek to increase the level of net earnings. The ratio can be calculated in two principal alternatives:

  - net earnings (pre- or post-tax) to capital employed;
  - net earnings to net operating assets (NOA). The definition of net operating assets is that of net assets but excluding cash or overdraft borrowings. In terms of operating efficiency, the NOA test may be the more relevant. Both the absolute relativity and the trend over a period of years are significant.

The profit and loss account

A comparison of the net worth of a company from one year to the next as shown in the two balance sheets discloses whether the company has made a profit or not. If it has, the net worth will have increased, subject to making adjustments, such as for the introduction of new capital or the payment of dividends. The profit and loss account sets out to show how this has been done. From the company's sales turnover will be deducted all the expenses incurred in order to achieve the turnover, the net difference between the two representing the profit (or loss) for the year.

The expenses should be identified as *variable* if they rise or fall in relationship to turnover, or *fixed* if, on the whole, they do not move in the short term in any direct relationship to turnover. This distinction is very important.

A business operating with high fixed costs is more vulnerable because it will take time to adjust to any reduction in turnover. On the other hand, once turnover exceeds the level of fixed costs, the level of profitability will be high. For this purpose, net revenue to the company, that is, gross revenue less variable costs, is more meaningful. It is this amount which is available to pay the fixed costs.

As with the balance sheet, the notes to the accounts must be read in order to appreciate the accounting policies which have been applied in the preparation of the profit and loss account, and to remember that the account is likely to be based on the historic cost convention, thus not reflecting changes in the domestic value of sterling.

Reading the profit and loss account

- The movement in turnover from one year to another is significant (but do not overlook inflationary or exchange influences to measure real change).
- The ratio of gross profit to turnover is known as the gross margin. Adequacy and consistency of gross margin is of the greatest importance.
- The ratio of net profit on ordinary activities to turnover is known as the net margin. This is the acid test of trading. Adequacy of net profit shows the basic health of the business and provides the resource from which to pay tax and dividends, and retentions for investment and future growth.
- The ratio of stock turnover is calculated by dividing the cost of goods sold by the average level of stocks. Stock turnover should be rapid, thus reducing the amount of capital locked up in the business. Stock turnover rates differ very substantially from one business to another. In this connection mention should be made of the effectiveness of many Japanese manufacturers who base their stocks and work-in-progress at an absolutely minimum level through the most rigid control of inward supply and in-factory

Typical profit and loss account

A typical profit and loss account based on Format 1 in Schedule 4 to the Companies Act 1985 would be set out as follows:

Profit and Loss Account
for the year ended . . . . 19...

	Notes	19..	19.. (previous year)
		£	£
Turnover			
Cost of sales		(_____)	(_____)
Gross profit (loss)			
Distribution costs		( )	( )
Administrative expenses		( )	( )
Other operating income		_____	_____
Operating profit			
Income from shares in group companies			
Income from shares in associated companies			
Income from other fixed asset investments			
Other interest receivable and similar income			
Amounts written off investments		( )	( )
Interest payable and similar charges		(_____)	(_____)
Profit (loss) on ordinary activities before taxation			
Tax on profit (loss) on ordinary activities		_____	_____
Profit (loss) on ordinary activities after taxation			
Extraordinary items (after taxation)		_____	_____
Profit (loss) for the year, after taxation			
Dividends paid and proposed		_____	_____
Amount transferred to (from) reserves		========	========

movements for immediate manufacturing purposes, now usually known as 'just in time'.

- Sales and profit per employee. As the employment strength has to be disclosed, it is possible to calculate these two significant ratios and to observe their trends. So far as possible make the calculation on average full-time employee head count.

- The most valuable indicator for comparative purposes is that of the earnings per share. Earnings can be expressed before or after taxation, but generally the post-tax figure should be regarded as more valuable since it is the profit ultimately available to shareholder interests. The basis of the post-tax profit should be made clear, since it can be calculated by reference to the actual tax charge or to a notional charge based on the standard tax rate. The number of shares in issue should be calculated by taking the weighted average throughout the financial year.

In the case of quoted companies, the stock market price of a share related to the earnings per share discloses the price/earnings ratio (the P/E ratio). It will be observed that, for a variety of factors but predominantly future prospects, the ratio can be as high as 40 or 50 or as low as single figures. From this share price can therefore be calculated the total market capitalisation of the company by multiplying the price by the number of shares in issue. It should not be expected that the market valuation will equate to the capital employed as shown in the balance sheet. The perception that the underlying assets of the company may be worth more than the valuation by the stock market can lead to take-over bids, intended to release the full underlying potential value of the company's assets either by merger into an existing business or to break up and sell off discrete parts of the target company.

Extraordinary and exceptional items

The 1985 Companies Act and Statements of Standard Accounting Practice (SSAPs) require that income or expenditure which is not of an ordinary trading nature shall be identified and reported separately. This ensures that the profit or loss on 'ordinary' activities is correctly disclosed.

An *extraordinary item* has been defined as one which is derived from events or transactions outside the ordinary activities of the business, being both material and not expected to recur frequently or regularly. Taxation related to extraordinary amounts is charged or credited in arriving at the amount.

Exceptional items, on the other hand, are those items which, while deriving from events or transactions that fall within the ordinary activities of the company, need to be disclosed separately by virtue of their unusual nature, size or incidence. The related taxation is not specifically attached to the exceptional item: it forms part of the normal taxation charge on ordinary activities. Although separated to allow proper understanding of the true results of trading, extraordinary items nevertheless directly affect the balance sheet, since they are taken into account when arriving at the increase or decrease in the reserves shown in the balance sheet. It may be necessary to look beyond any particular year fully to appreciate their significance.

Funds flow

In addition to the balance sheet and profit and loss account, there must be a funds flow statement, except in the case of enterprises with a turnover of less than £25,000 per annum.

The funds flow statement effectively links the balance sheet and profit and loss accounts to cash flows. Its principal features are to demonstrate the source and application of funds arising from:

- operations of the business;
- changes in working capital by component;
- acquisition and disposal of fixed and other non-current assets;
- movements in short-term, medium-term and long-term loans;
- dividends paid;
- changes in share capital.

The sum of these changes will reveal the movement in net liquid funds. An illustration of a funds flow statement is shown in Appendix 2. The flow of cash through the business is a very significant indicator of financial health.

Forecasts

The financier is more interested in the future position than the historic, since the justification for the financing and the company's ability to service any additional funding will be in the future.

The historic position will be shown by the year-end balance sheet, the profit and loss account for the period (usually a year) ending on that date and a corresponding funds flow statement.

In respect of the period since the year end, the financier will expect to see management accounts and a forecast of the current year's results based on the latest management accounts. For the period beyond the current year, he will expect to see:

- for the immediate forthcoming year, a detailed monthly or quarterly profit and loss statement, cash flows for the same periods and a forecast balance sheet at the period end;
- for at least the next following year, and preferably three years, the same type of information, but stated on a quarterly, half yearly or annual basis.

The forecasts can only be considered in relation to the assumptions and plans which are the basis for the financial forecasts. This therefore means that a credible business plan must be prepared to justify the financial statements. The contents and preparation of this business plan will be considered in more detail in Chapter 2.

Taxation

Before leaving these general considerations, mention must be made (as in almost every facet of commercial life) of taxation.

In this respect, among others, the question of company location must be taken into account. If a company is located in England, English law applies; if located in Scotland, Scottish law will apply, but the same UK tax legislation will be applicable to either location. But if the location is outside the UK, the company will escape UK corporate taxation only if the seat of management and control is actually outside the UK.

Moreover, some thought should be given at an early stage to the likely future sources of profits and in which countries substantial business activities are envisaged. And from these considerations, advice should be taken – both commercially and taxation-wise – as to the most appropriate vehicle through which to conduct overseas trading. This may be a company or a branch. The precise status will be affected by UK and local taxation rules.

Thus, at an early stage, professional advice must be taken as to the relative implications of alternative courses. Such comparisons are complex. In the United States, for example, not only Federal and State taxes must be considered but in some cases local taxes as well.

One other point: if substantial overseas trading is contemplated, with income flowing to the UK holding company through dividend distributions, such income will be treated as investment income in the UK. In the case of a 'close' company (broadly one controlled by five or fewer persons) UK tax law requires that investment income be distributed to shareholders who, of course, may be taxed on it. Trading income, however, is treated differently and does not have to be distributed.

There are other considerations. For example, dividend distributions in the UK are subject to advanced corporation tax (ACT). This tax may only be recovered against the payment of mainstream corporation tax on corporate income (including, since 1987, capital gains tax). It may be that there is insufficient mainstream corporation tax to allow full offset of ACT, which is then irrecoverable and effectively adds to the taxation burden.

Thought should be given at an early stage to the taxation consequences for individuals. Such considerations may influence the location of the company and/or the residence of employees or shareholders. One of the most difficult areas is that of taxation for employees who are also either shareholders or potential shareholders, for example, through share options. The Inland Revenue attitude will be to regard benefits from share ownership as employment related and therefore to tax them as income. Or it may be that an employee is transferring rights to the company – for example, the assignment of patent benefits. The Inland Revenue will wish to establish the basis of transfer, that it is a fair arm's length valuation, and whether there are other benefits associated with the transaction which may give rise to potential tax liabilities.

Right from the beginning, therefore, tax planning for the company and for employees and owners should figure high on the agenda. This will certainly apply to new company formation and business start-ups, and proper provision must be made for the professional fees.

Professional advisers

The financier will need to know what professional advice has been taken by the directors. He will take into account the presumed quality of that advice.

The accountants and lawyers (both of whom will be concerned with taxation) are the two constant factors in any business, together with the company bankers. In addition, there may be pension fund advisers, actuaries, surveyors, insurance brokers, employee benefit advisers and consulting engineers; possibly marketing consultants, advertising and PR agencies too. Where appropriate, it will be helpful to quote the names of any consultants and advisers used by the company.

Conclusion

All directors must acquire a basic understanding of company accounts, the conventions used in their preparation, the importance of the notes which are essential to a proper interpretation of them and, above all, an ability to read the figures and their implications for the business.

In particular, carefully selected ratios should be reviewed regularly, their trends observed and compared with predetermined norms set by management. The latest company accounts are an essential element in the preparation of a financial case, representing a firm historical base of actual achievement, together with a forecast of future expectations, prepared on a conservative basis.

Chapter 2
The Financial Proposal

Introduction

The basic requirements to support an application for funds are the same, whether borrowing and/or capital raising is involved.

In the case of lending, the lender is concerned about two fundamental issues. Can the loan be adequately serviced and can it be repaid in full in accordance with the loan agreement? With capital, the investor is also concerned about two issues. Can he expect his investment to be serviced by a continuous and increasing stream of dividends and can he expect an increasing value in the investment with an ability to realise it readily in due course?

Basic requirements

A proposal must therefore be formulated by the company with the purpose of satisfying these key requirements. To do so, the following will be necessary as a minimum:

- Details of the board of the company and its key management.
- The latest year-end accounts.
- The latest management accounts, including a year-end profit forecast and balance sheet.
- A business plan.
- A financial forecast for at least two years, possibly up to five years. This may be incorporated in the business plan.
- Projected year-end balance sheets.
- Corresponding cash flow forecasts.

It is likely that the financial proposal will be set out in a covering note, but it may be contained in a separate schedule to the 'package'.

Where a company has an established business relationship, for example with a bank, it is not necessary to repeat information already on bank files, such as the Memorandum and Articles of Association and the latest accounts. As confidence grows, the relationship will become less formal. Nevertheless, the basic homework should always be done to satisfy the company making the proposal that the request is soundly based and justified.

It is unlikely that the Memorandum and Articles of Association will be submitted in the initial stages, but they will be examined at some time during the course of routine legal work. It is necessary, therefore, that the proposer is aware of the principal provisions in both documents, in particular those relating to the share capital and shareholders' rights attaching to each class of share and, in the case of borrowings, the relevant conditions and borrowing limits imposed on the directors in the Articles of Association.

Contingency planning

Careful consideration will always need to be given to the most appropriate type of finance required by the company, and the relative cost of alternative methods. The raising of any finance from third parties is a step only to be taken with responsibility and a proper regard for the moral obligation entered into. There must be no doubt on the part of the applicant, barring some unforeseen event, that the business projections can reasonably be met. Raising money is all about reputation and confidence: memories are very long. It will frequently be the case that professional advice is taken before any approaches are made. That will be essential for any public offering or the equivalent of a prospectus, as will be seen in Chapter 6.

It is wise to ensure that there is provision for an adequate contingency sum in estimating the amount required. It will be most unusual if plans, however carefully prepared, work out precisely as envisaged.

Cash flow is the life-blood of a business. If actual events deviate from plan, this will rapidly become evident in the cash situation. There are usually two reasons for cash forecasts going astray. One relates to time. For example, enough time may not have been allowed for the construction of buildings or the bringing of products to a marketable state. Consideration must be given to the key time elements in the plans and reasonable estimates made of the likely financial consequences if there is slippage, and the actions that may be taken to limit damage to the plans and financial calculations. The second aspect relates to failure to achieve forecast revenues, margins or expense levels. There are bound to be a limited number of sensitive points which can significantly affect financial expectations. The planning process should identify these points and propose solutions to contain the cash flow damage which is likely to result. For these reasons, it is wise:

- To propose business plans on a prudent and conservative basis and not assume that every event will happen exactly as planned. Because it is part of the nature of businessmen and entrepreneurs to be optimistic, all assumptions should be carefuly challenged for probability.
- To include a generous contingency sum in the financial proposal to allow for the many unplanned events which always occur, despite a conservative approach in the basic assumptions.
- To prepare alternative solutions, based on, say, 'conservative' and 'probable' out-turns. Both can be included in the financial proposal. It can then be seen that the directors are taking care not to pretend that the out-turn can be forecast with great accuracy.

It is embarrassing at best, difficult or impossible at worst, to return to the well for another drink based on inadequate foresight. It damages that crucial factor – confidence – and raises questions about good judgement.

The board of directors

In the formulation of a business project, the individuals who form the board of directors are far and away the greatest factor in the success of the business. And the composition of the board will be looked at very carefully by any person or institution approached for funding. This cannot be stressed too strongly, and it is particularly demonstrated by the care with which the board is presented when a company seeks a listing on the market.

The board will be scrutinised for:

- integrity;
- balance of executive and non-executive directors;
- business acumen, based on previous performance;
- balance of skills and experience;
- independence of character and view;
- motivation;
- its chairman;
- its chief executive.

All company policies and directions stem from the board. The board must have the ability to work together, to formulate and execute business plans; to appoint (or ensure that those responsible appoint) managers of high quality; to drive the whole business in the required direction; and to set the tone for the company. Responsibility for success or failure lies at the boardroom door and nowhere else.

Because total responsibility for the conduct of the company can only lie with the board, the individuals who comprise it and the perception of their competence as a team working together will be of the utmost importance to a financier. The two pivotal positions are those of chairman and managing director.

Chairman

The chairman is appointed by the board to preside over it. He may be full-time and perform executive functions in addition to his role as chairman, or he may be only part-time and non-executive. The relationship between the roles of chairman and managing director varies enormously from company to company and must be the subject of agreement by the board. Usually, the chairman has responsibility for external corporate relations, which include shareholders and financial institutions.

The managing director

The board almost invariably appoints one of its directors to be responsible to the board for the overall conduct of the business, subject to the policy of the board. This person may be known as the managing director or the chief executive. Whatever the title, the board must define the duties, responsibilities and limits of authority which the position entails.

The managing director is the principal channel through which the board conducts business. The appointment (and sometimes removal) of the managing director is therefore crucial. This is one reason to prefer, even in quite small companies, the separation of the role of the chairman from that of the principal manager. They have different duties, and board meetings are generally more effective if there is an independent chairman. Of course, there are many highly effective companies which have combined the role of chairman and chief executive, but the modern tendency is towards separation.

The principal tasks of the managing director are:

- to implement the policies of the board;
- to achieve the objectives agreed with the board;
- to recommend policy to the board;
- to co-ordinate and direct the work of the other executive directors;

- to ensure that the board and, in particular, the non-executive directors are kept properly informed about the progress of the business.

Where the role of managing director is combined with that of chairman, it is clearly very powerful. With a separate chairman there is effectively a 'court of appeal' for disputes arising at senior level. And if there is dissatisfaction with the performance of the managing director, it is far more difficult to apply objective tests and obtain the views of the non-executive directors if the managing director is also the chairman. The power to bring about change is also seriously limited in such cases because non-executive directors tend to be invited on the initiative of the chairman.

While the chairman's overall responsibility is likely to include banking relations, the routine contact may be with the managing director and/or the finance director. The managing director will be the central figure involved in any financial proposal to the bank or other financial house.

Chairman and managing director must work very closely together, meeting frequently – perhaps daily – so that they are both completely in touch with current events and can discuss them as they happen. With a non-executive chairman the working relationship is likely to be less close, with less frequent meetings and discussions. Whatever the working method, it is important that these two critical people are very much on the same wavelength, leading the team of directors in a constructive way.

Finance director

The third executive director who should be specially mentioned is the finance director. He will frequently report directly to the chairman and carry overall responsibility for the good housekeeping of the company's financial affairs. He can expect to participate actively in all major decisions since they all have financial and taxation implications. The position of the finance director is not without difficulty. Not only does it require professional competence of a high order, but also commercial skills and the strength of character necessary to stand up to the many pressures to 'bend the rules' in the interests of presenting improved results. To perform those tasks and yet remain respected as a working colleague requires special qualities, not the least of which is the ability to communicate and persuade. If a single director is the repository of corporate 'conscience', it is the finance director.

Non-executive directors

Directors who are not performing an executive role in the company are usually referred to as non-executive directors: they carry the same responsibilities as any other director.

Their value lies essentially in their independence, without which they have no place on the board. In addition, they should bring to the board a new and broader perspective, and should be capable of judging the performance of executive directors. They must have integrity and a willingness to express opinions which may not necessarily be welcomed by all other members. They must also have access to all key information if the company is to benefit fully from their ability to contribute to board discussions.

The chairman has a special relationship with the non-executive directors. They are able to express an opinion about external matters likely to affect the company, frequently with a broader range of experience to draw upon than the executive directors. If questions arise about the composition of the board, or the progress of the company, the chairman will almost certainly seek their advice.

Carefully selected non-executive directors enhance the quality of debate at board level and contribute to the company's performance. The financier will be particularly interested in the quality and experience of the non-executive directors who are in the best position to exercise a strong independent influence at board level.

Management

The key to running a successful business is the creation of an effective management team. This is the prime responsibility of the board. The board's appointment of the managing director is crucial, but it should also take an interest in the appointment of the principal subordinate managers.

The financier will be interested in the qualifications of the key managers, and the depth of the organisational structure of the business.

Management accounts

A business cannot be effectively managed without regular navigational aids, one of which is the early preparation of accurate monthly management accounts. The board must make clear the format it requires and the routine timetable for submission. The accounts will be supported by the identification of key ratios, designed to monitor the essential pressure points and their trends.

The latest management accounts will be required to support the financial case. Among other things, they will disclose:

- The cumulative results since the beginning of the financial year.
- A latest year-end projection.
- A comparison with the budget which willl have been prepared before the commencement of the year as part of the business plan.
- The previous year's results.
- The key ratios.

The management accounts package should include:

- profit and loss account
- balance sheet
- cash flow statement
- order and revenue analysis by principal products
- order backlog by principal products, and margins.

The balance sheet and cash flow statements will highlight the movements in working capital. This is a sensitive indicator and must always be kept under regular review.

The business plan

The real interest of any financier is, of course, not the past, but the future. The accounts for a preceding year, and the management accounts to date, provide a background of considerable value which will be carefully analysed to determine the financial health of the business. They are also the most significant evidence of achievement.

The business plan, an essential ingredient in any financial proposal, addresses the future. It should cover at least three years, preferably five, and the immediately forthcoming year in greater detail. Its financial starting point will be firmly based on the latest accounts, or management accounts, as appropriate.

The purpose of the business plan is:

- to establish the corporate objectives;
- to define the strategy to be followed to achieve the objectives;
- to develop the methods by which the strategy is to be achieved;
- to build a financial plan, in particular projected profit and loss accounts, balance sheets at year ends (quarterly for the first year of the plan), and cash flows. Any assumptions are important and should be explicitly stated.

A business plan is not written specifically as a financial presentation. Its preparation should form part of the regular operations of the company, and be the subject of agreement and commitment by the board as a whole.

The first year of the plan is usually called the 'budget year' and will normally be prepared on a monthly basis to permit more reality in the planning and provide a comparative base against which to measure future actual performance.

A business plan, properly prepared, is a comprehensive piece of work and requires considerable effort from the management if it is to be credible. While the financial plan is, of course, an essential element, it is not the only, or even the main, purpose. That purpose is to work out how the company will achieve its stated objectives in the first year in detail, and in subsequent years in sufficient outline to establish the thrust of the business; the problems and opportunities for the company and how it is proposed they will be accommodated; the marketing and sales plans; and the manpower requirements. Appendix 3 outlines the main structure of a fully developed business plan. Such detail will not necessarily be appropriate in all cases, but it will help to underline the comprehensive approach which, in principle, is always necessary.

The financial proposal

While the full plan could be submitted to the financier, it is almost certainly better, at any rate in the initial approaches, to provide a shorter document. The aim will be to provide all the information required to allow rapid assimilation of the business proposal. If further information is required in due course, it will be easily and readily available.

It is suggested by way of illustration that the proposal should be structured along the following lines:

- Table of contents of the presentation.
- Definition of terms.
- Names of directors and key managers together with brief details of their qualifications.
- Names of professional advisers.
- Introduction to, and perhaps also a summary of, the business proposal.
- History of the business.
- Summary of the market in which the business intends to operate.
- Outline of the operation and methods to be followed by the business.

- The corporate structure.
- Management and organisation structure.
- Financial plan.
- Uses to which proceeds will be applied.
- Assessment of the risks.
- Future dividend policy.
- Plans for listing on the Stock Exchange or Unlisted Securities Market.
- Proposal to the potential financial source.
- List of appendices (in which much of the supporting detail may be included).

The following requirements must be satisfied by the proposal:

- Sufficient total funding to meet the estimated requirements, which must therefore embrace:
  - capital expenditure
  - working capital requirements
  - provision for operating losses incurred during the development of products and market entry and development costs. Sufficient consideration is frequently not given to what factors influence the buyer and who actually makes the buying decision. This often results in a longer lead time in effecting sales than is provided in the revenue forecasts. Such delays may be partly influenced by the very fact that the business has yet to reach a mature stage.
  - a contingency provision. Some unexpected event, usually adverse, often characterises young business.
- A sound relationship of borrowing to shareholders' funds.
- Sufficient earnings to permit adequate cover for interest payable on borrowed monies and to make a return on the equity capital an attractive reward for the risks involved.
- Attention should also be given to possible future financial requirements. It may influence the structuring of the current financial requirement.

Particular mention should be made of the importance of the cash flow forecast. It will disclose the period results and cumulative position. This is the easiest way to establish the maximum financial need and when it occurs. The forecast will also determine whether this is a short-term bank requirement or a long-term lending situation. Naturally, it will be affected by capital requirements, which should be distinguished from operational cash movements. The first marker is thus put down as to the

41

nature of the funding requirement and therefore the most appropriate source to meet it.

There is no ideal length, but in principle, the aim should be to submit a well-written, concise but comprehensive proposal. Financiers are busy people and have many propositions to consider. Clarity of message and requirements will help the case. This point cannot be emphasised too strongly. Financiers are inundated with proposals. It is critical that your particular proposal is sufficiently interesting at the first 'sieving' stage to deserve further attention. If it is not, it is difficult to get back in the queue. It is somewhat sobering to know that rather less than 5 per cent of proposals submitted to some financiers will result in a favourable investment decision.

The chairman or managing director and the finance director will be most involved in presenting the case and providing detailed answers. They should try to anticipate and to prepare suitable responses. These exchanges are important in making the financier confident that the proposer knows what he is doing and can be trusted.

Working capital

The make-up of working capital was considered in Chapter 1. Its importance cannot be overemphasised. There are two particularly diffi-cult circumstances. The first, when a business is operating at a loss; the second, when it is expanding fast. If, for example, working capital normally represents 25 per cent of turnover, then for every increase in turnover of £100,000 there will be an increased capital requirement of £25,000. This will need constant control if dangers are to be avoided.

The factors which are most relevant to the level of working capital include:

- The nature of the business
  Broadly, the nearer a business is to operating on a cash basis, the lower the working capital. The larger the production period involved (such as in a manufacturing business) the greater will be the investment in working capital.
- The extent of management control over the individual items making up the working capital
  Essentially, that involves:
  - strong credit control, to limit the number of days of uncollected debts;
  - rigid stock control, through every element of the stockholding process;

- strong control of cash disbursements and regular forecasting of requirements;
- strong control of creditor payments.

- Operating losses
  Cash resources will inevitably be adversely affected by operating losses.
- Operating profits
  Profitable business should just as inevitably result in increased positive cash flows. Therefore, the aim to raise net profit margins (without other detrimental consequences) should be a consistent management aim. By one means or another, this will essentially be achieved through increasing gross contributions and reducing actually, or relatively, the fixed costs.
- Expanding business
  If turnover is growing, it can be expected that demands for working capital will grow too. It may not be possible to finance this increased investment fully from internal resources or bank facilities. A fast-growing business will probably need access to increased capital resources from time to time.

In the case of public issues, the accountants and directors are required to examine carefully their future needs for working capital, and to be satisfied that they can be met. Failure to finance working capital requirements, characterised by an inability to make payments as they fall due, will bring about business failure and is almost certainly the most common cause of it. For that reason, top management must take a close interest in the composition and control of its working capital requirements.

Future financing

One of the principal purposes of the business plan is to ensure that the financial requirements to support the intended objectives and strategies are identified.

It is not good enough to identify the immediate requirements or, indeed, those for the year ahead. The financier will wish to understand the full implications of the proposal, and what further funding demands are likely to arise in the foreseeable future, say in the period three to five years ahead.

It is not unusual to envisage funding on a staged basis, particularly in the case of young development projects, with further funding to become available if the company achieves agreed targets, frequently referred to as milestones.

If the company is developing satisfactorily, and further funding is envisaged, it cannot be expected that the company valuation will remain constant. For example, with a young company, the equity funding will probably be introduced at *par*, ie at the face value of the share. Later, there will be a premium attaching to the shares reflecting business progress. There may be conversion options attaching to loans, ie the right to convert loans into share capital; the price at which such conversion takes place will need careful consideration since it is an event which may take place some time in the future.

In any case, additional tranches of finance introduced in the future will almost certainly be at a higher price, based on the calculated company valuation at the time of the funding. This is perfectly normal and may well be anticipated in the original financing agreement.

Exit

The proposal to the financier for a non-quoted company should make it clear how it is intended the investment can be realised. No financier – or private investor for that matter – will be happy without knowing the exit route in due course, and when that might be anticipated.

Of course, it is not possible to know exactly what circumstances will arise several years ahead. Nevertheless, the objectives of the principal parties can and should be made clear. If the plan is, at the appropriate time, to seek quotation on the Unlisted Securities Market (USM) or a full listing on the Stock Exchange, it is likely that the prospects and financial situation will support other methods of realisation. Thus merger, take-over or indeed other routes, such as a reverse take-over, ie the acquisition of the shares of one company in exchange for the shares of a quoted company, with the result that the first company has effectively achieved a share quotation, will be feasible.

The requirements in all cases are, therefore:

- a progressive record
- a soundly financed business
- a competent board of directors
- future prospects of continuing success.

It is important to ensure that this matter receives proper consideration and is included in the business plan or financial proposal put forward to the financier.

Conclusion

This chapter has addressed the principles involved in the formulation of a soundly based financial proposal. This requirement applies whether borrowing or capital is the preferred solution.

It is quite likely that the sequence of events will be along the following lines. First, an initial approach to generate interest and receptivity. Second, the submission of the proposal along the lines outlined in this chapter. This is likely to be followed by a discussion to allow the financier to cross-examine the proposer on the proposition and his confidence in its achievement. More detailed work may then follow, particularly if long-term capital is being raised or new business developed. This may well extend to site visits, meetings with the directors and selected managers, so that the financier can get a real feel for the business and form his independent views as to the probability of success.

Thereafter, there will be a decision and, if favourable, a response in principle by the financier outlining the main conditions which will attach to the financial arrangment. If that is acceptable to the proposer, detailed legal and documentary work will follow to bring the matter to a satisfactory conclusion. Experience shows that, time after time, the extensive work involved requires more time and effort than is anticipated. Therefore, it is advisable to allow a substantial contingency in the planning period. In the case of start-ups or difficult propositions several financial sources may need to be approached before a mutually satisfactory solution emerges. Some venture capital proposals take more than a year to be brought to the starting blocks. That is, perhaps, unusual. What is normal is the considerable time and effort required from senior management.

Chapter 3
Borrowings

Introduction

The sources of funding for any business, as identified in Chapter 1, are either shareholders' funds or borrowings. There is, in fact, a third source of funding provided by government grants, which will be considered as a separate issue. In this chapter, the more general types of borrowing available to a business are considered, and some of the factors which are likely to affect the type and amount of borrowing to be made.

It might be helpful in the first place to establish some of the general principles affecting borrowed monies. It must be remembered that those lending money to a business are concerned about two key issues:

- Will the interest charge (and any other fees) be paid regularly in accordance with the terms of the loan?
- Will the money lent be repaid in accordance with the loan agreement?

The bank or other lender will inevitably take a cautious view. Financial institutions must themselves be governed by prudent conduct because substantial parts of the monies they lend are obtained from third parties, such as loans to them or deposits with them. They will be conforming to strict rules about the proportions of their assets lent and the proportions of their loans to their own capital resources. For these reasons, banks will apply their own criteria to financial statements in determining the amounts they are prepared to lend, and satisfy themselves that the projected results of the borrower will amply cover the interest payments and principal repayments, even given adverse trading circumstances. Banks, therefore, follow strict internal credit procedures and internal approval levels depending on the size and nature of the intended loan.

Financial institutions normally work on tight margins. Any bank which must fund all its borrowed monies in the financial markets and does not enjoy interest-free current accounts may work on margins of ½ per cent or less. Clearing banks do enjoy some interest-free current accounts, but have to support a substantial branch structure to obtain them. Either way, the cost of failure to recover loans is substantial and damaging; effectively, it must be funded by the bank from its own capital resources with, therefore, a knock-on effect on its subsequent ability to make loans because of a deteriorating ratio of capital to lending.

The banker's position

Before considering what the business wants or would like, it may be helpful to understand some of the factors which are likely to govern the bank's lending activities. Often more is expected of the banker than is reasonable. It must be accepted that the overriding interest of any banker is to retain confidence, for without it the banking business simply cannot be conducted.

A number of Acts of Parliament are directly relevant to the conduct of UK banking, the principal being the 1987 Banking Act. The 1958 Prevention of Fraud (Investments) Act (to be replaced by the Financial Services Act) and the 1974 Consumer Credit Act relate particularly to the 'money' business. The Companies Act 1985 is also applicable, as is the Insolvency Act 1986.

The Bank of England is responsible for the supervision of the Banking Act, and other relevant legislation. It alone is authorised to approve any deposit-taking institution conducting business in the UK.

The company must have a minimum of £1 million in respect of capital and reserve. Each director, controller and manager must satisfy the Bank of England he is a fit and proper person. The board of the company must also include non-executive directors to the satisfaction of the Bank.

The Bank will require to be satisfied about several significant criteria, including:

- integrity and skill
- prudent conduct
- adequacy of assets
- bad debt provisions
- accounting and control systems.

The Bank of England exercises its supervisory role, where appropriate, through the submission by banks, on a regular basis, of a number of reports in standard format. The Bank manages the system on a flexible basis (as opposed to the banking supervision in some other countries) and establishes criteria which are considered appropriate to each particular bank. The reporting procedures are strengthened by regular discussion between the bank and the supervisory authority.

The adequacy of a bank's capital (stringently defined) in relation to its creditors and its loan customers are the two fundamental relationships which govern the limits to which a bank can trade, viewed in a group context.

The 'risk asset ratio' is the most important test; it relates the capital base to the loan portfolio, weighted in accordance with a scale which increases with risk. A bank seeks to ensure a planned maturity in its assets, with a prudent spread of loans by industrial sector and geographical territory. The resulting weighted total is then related to the defined base capital. It is probable that a ratio of some 12 per cent or above may be considered acceptable.

A number of guidance papers establishing a carefully constructed control system have been issued by the Bank of England. They deal with such matters as the measurement of capital, foreign currency exposure, the measurement of liquidity, off-balance-sheet business and large exposures.

It is against this background that the banker will approach his potential borrower. He will therefore seek to understand the borrower's business and his financial state, and to monitor the progress of the business through regular management reporting and in particular cash flows, together with periodic discussion with his customer. The banker will be as interested in key ratios as the business manager. He will be very interested in liquidity, particularly in relation to the make-up of working capital into its primary constituents of stocks, debtors and creditors. He will want to know about the company gearing and its potential liabilities. It is always wise to keep your banker fully informed of good and bad news. No businessman welcomes shocks, least of all the banker.

Some principles of borrowing

There are certain general rules which should be recognised by any borrower. No doubt there will be occasions when the general rules will vary, but they should always be considered most carefully in the light of all the circumstances:

- Match borrowings to assets or, put another way, do not borrow 'short' and invest 'long'. It is inappropriate to finance the acquisition of fixed assets by bank overdraft finance because such finance is essentially repayable on demand and, if called, could cause difficulties for the borrower.

It may be mentioned that property developments may be financed by short-term bank borrowing during construction, but when completed, the short-term will be replaced by longer-term borrowing. This may be effected by the developer himself, or the party to whom the completed development is sold. In the case of substantial property developers, a multi-option facility may be arranged to meet the need for flexibility.

- Borrowings made in a foreign currency should only be used for investing in assets of the same currency. Because of the unpredictability of exchange rate movements, a currency borrowing used for investment in a different currency immediately opens up an exchange rate risk, adding an area of uncertainty which is far better avoided, although currency 'hedging' may be arranged.

- There must be a prudent relationship between borrowings and capital. A company with no borrowings or a low rate of borrowing to capital is known as having 'low gearing'. The reverse situation is a 'highly geared' company, having borrowings of, say, 1:2 and approaching 1:1. The attractiveness of high gearing is to enhance the return on capital because interest on borrowing should be a lesser burden than the costs of capital. But interest is a fixed cost (even though interest rates may vary), whereas dividends are paid only if earned.

It is, therefore, imprudent to saddle the company earnings with too high a level of fixed interest cost because of the sensitivity of net earnings to relatively modest reductions in turnover. This is particularly the case if fixed costs form a high proportion of company overheads.

Consider an example:

Turnover	100
Gross margin	40
Fixed overheads	35
Net margin	5
If turnover drops by	3%
Gross margin is less by	1.2 (ie at 40%)
Net margin becomes	3.8 (ie 5-1.2)
ie a reduction in net margin of	24%

There may be occasions when borrowings form a much higher

ratio than should normally be contemplated. For example, in start-up situations loans and capital may be virtually indistinguishable in the early periods; they are both high-risk finance, and the lender is often rewarded by a stake in the capital or perhaps an option to convert part of the loan into equity at the lender's discretion.

An alternative method of expressing the borrowing risk is to relate borrowings to the assets employed. This is known as the gearing ratio. A broad classification might be:

Ratio	Percentage
Low	6–20
Medium	20–40
High	over 40

For the purpose of establishing the borrowing risk, all borrowings need to be taken into account. They will therefore include:
- current liabilities (even if netted off in the balance sheet against current assets, but excluding trade creditors);
- bank overdrafts;
- loans up to five years;
- loans over five years;
- debentures.

The existence of preference share capital causes some difficulty, particularly if it is redeemable. It is neither equity nor borrowing. If it is not redeemable, it should be treated as capital. However, if it is redeemable the effect of redemption will be to reduce ordinary shareholders' free reserves by allocating to a capital redemption reserve fund an amount equivalent to the monies applied in the redemption. Whereas some analysts will treat redeemable preference shares as borrowings for ratio purposes, it may be acceptable to treat them as 'neutral'.

A banker making ratio calculations may well ignore intangible assets and make his ratio calculations on 'net tangible assets'. In some cases, this prudent approach can make the ratio calculation very tough.

It will be appreciated that shareholders' capital includes the reserves attributable to ordinary shareholders including undistributed profits, share premium, revaluation reserves and captial redemption reserves. In the case of group accounts, the 'minority interests' may or may not be treated as capital for ratio purposes.

An illustration of the effects of gearing may be helpful (see page 52). Company B debt/equity ratio is 67 per cent and gearing ratio 40 per cent.

Funding Your Business

Funding	Company A £	Company B £
Issued ordinary shares of £1 each	1,000,000	600,000
Loans 12.5%		400,000
Capital employed	1,000,000	1,000,000

	High	Medium	Low	High	Medium	Low
Rate of return on employed capital	35%	20%	5%	35%	20%	5%
Profits before tax and interest	350,000	200,000	50,000	350,000	200,000	50,000
Interest	–	–	–	50,000	50,000	50,000
Profits after interest	350,000	200,000	50,000	300,000	150,000	–
Taxation 35%	122,500	70,000	17,500	105,000	52,500	–
Profit after Tax	227,500	130,000	32,500	195,000	97,500	–
Earnings per share (p)	*22.75*	*13.00*	*3.25*	*32.5*	*16.25*	*NIL*

52

Characteristics

Some or all of the following characteristics will be present in borrowing agreements:

- The period of the borrowing. If the borrowing is effectively an overdraft facility, there will be a right by the lender to require repayment on demand. In other cases, there will be an 'event of default' clause, allowing acceleration of repayment should a default occur.
- The rate of interest and various types of facility fee (and the frequency of charging them). Non-use fees may also be payable ie a percentage per annum on the unused facilities from time to time within the credit limit.
- The security given by the borrower (or some third party on his behalf).
- The ability of the lender to transfer/assign/subparticipate the loan to some third party.
- The flexibility, if any, which exists to vary the terms of the arrangement.
- Rights to the lender to convert the loan or part of it into ordinary share capital, or other forms of reward to the banker for funding a particular transaction, such as profit sharing.
- The subordination of borrowings to other creditors, ie that other creditors have priority of repayment against the subordinated loan (which arrangement may tie in with the structure of a security package).
- The ability of a borrower to move into other currencies, principally to reduce interest costs. But there will be currency/exchange risks in doing so.
- Restrictions on the borrower from making other borrowings, from disposing of assets, from changing the nature of its business, and giving security ('negative pledge') so long as the loan is outstanding.
- Events of default.

There will be restrictions on the directors' ability to exercise the company's borrowing powers in the Articles of Association. Borrowing powers are contained in the 'objects' clause of a company's Memorandum of Association along with its powers to give security, guarantees etc. There may also be restrictions in loan agreements.

If the borrowing is secured by a debenture, there will be a number of conditions in the debenture deed as to what the borrower may or may not do in relation to the charged assets.

Secured borrowings will either be fixed or specific on certain assets of the company, or 'floating' which means that the security extends to all the company's assets, including working capital which, in the nature of trading, is constantly changing, but will 'crystallise' on the particular assets of the company when enforcement occurs.

Rates of interest can also vary. One of the important factors affecting interest rates is the bank's credit rating of its customer. The rate of interest may be fixed for the whole period of the loan: more likely it will be variable, as a fixed margin over the lending bank's base rate or over a market rate such as LIBOR (the London inter-bank offered rate). Failure to meet an interest payment will usually trigger the lender's recovery rights against the borrower.

In many loan agreements, particularly those relating to bank over-drafts, there will be conditions with which the borrower must comply on an ongoing basis, such as in connection with the amounts invested in debtors and stocks, and other financial covenants. Normally the bank requires the borrower to submit management accounts on a regular basis in order to monitor the company's general progress (against its plans) and to satisfy itself that the working capital loan conditions are being complied with, and that the borrower's financial condition is not deter-iorating, for example a material adverse change in the borrower's assets, financial condition, business etc. In addition, the audited annual and semi-annual (unaudited) statements will be submitted to the bank.

Loans

Loans will usually fall most appropriately into the following categories:

Bank overdrafts
Essentially, these are suitable to provide working capital. The bank does not wish or intend bank overdraft facilities to become part of the 'core' borrowings of a long-term nature. The intention is to make available facilities to cover seasonal fluctuations in trade, or heavy investment in stocks which will be released during the trading year. They are repayable on demand. In any case, the bank may well not wish to see its overdraft wholly carrying the investment in net current assets. It will expect to see the company providing a reasonable proportion of working capital from its own resources.

Mention has already been made of the substantial demand for increasing sums for working capital as business expands. It is a potential danger point. If overdrafts are taking on the appearance of fixed loans, the bank will probably initiate discussions to convert some or all into a more permanent arrangement either by longer-term loans or the introduction of more shareholders' capital.

Acceptance credits

The practice of bills of exchange being accepted by a bank has led to the development of an acceptance credit facility as a normal method of raising finance as an alternative to, or combined with, an overdraft facility. Within an overall facility limit, which should normally be related to commercial trading activity, a company may draw bills on the bank for acceptance and subsequent discounting in the market, to be honoured by the bank for the account of its customer at maturity date. It is therefore the accepting bank which takes the primary risk for honouring the bill, and charges an acceptance commission in addition to the discount cost on the bank bill (which is known as such when endorsed by the bank). If bills are to be eligible for rediscount with the Bank of England, they have to be supported by an appropriate level of underlying trading activity. Those banks which may discount bills with the Bank of England are known as 'eligible banks'. This is, therefore, a very flexible complement to other facilities. The borrower has agreed with the accepting bank that it will pay the bank the amount which the bank must pay to the party presenting the bill at maturity. It will therefore show the liability for bills yet to mature under 'creditors' in the balance sheet.

Short-term loans

Say one to two years.

Revolving credit facilities

Advances for periods up to six months which have to be repaid at the end of the specified period but are then available for redrawing within the facility limit. Usually such an arrangement will be for periods between one and five years.

Medium-term loans

These usually fall within a two- to five-year term and are generally intended to match assets of corresponding life, or perhaps in connection with a restructuring of the balance sheet.

Loan repayments should roughly coincide with the depreciation or amortisation of the asset's useful life. The effect of such provisions is to retain corresponding amounts of cash; although a charge in the accounts, they do not represent a cash outgoing.

Long-term loans
Loans of more than five years fall into this category and are of similar intent to medium-term loans, ie to be matched against longer-term assets. In some cases – debentures for instance – there may be a term of 20 years, usually associated with freehold or long leasehold properties. Some long-term loans are intended to represent capital, eg perpetual or long-term debt which is subordinated, thus only ranking ahead of equity. Several banks have issued perpetual notes. Term loans will, among other conditions, provide for repayments during the term of the loan and, most probably, floating interest rates adjusted to current market levels at regular intervals. Floating interest rates are less likely to be appropriate in the case of long-term mortgages and debentures. Because they are long term, however, there are risks arising from interest rate movements which may be difficult to foresee when the obligation is incurred.

Multi-option facilities
These facilities are now becoming common for larger companies. They provide access to all types of borrowing, some of which may be used regularly, with the remainder being on a stand-by basis. They will often be made available by a syndicate of committed banks.

Cover

It has already been stated that the lender is concerned about the regular payment of interest and repayment of his capital. It is normal, as part of the lender's 'due diligence', to make calculations as to the adequacy of cover available, and projected to be available, in both respects.

The borrower, for his own safety, should be equally interested. The concept is similar to the calculations made with regard to the adequacy of after-tax profit cover for dividends. In that case the investor wishes to know how adequate the profits are to pay the expected dividends. If the distributions take nearly the whole of the available profit, ie approaching 100 per cent, the prudent investor will conclude that the dividend is too high and may not be sustained if there is any setback in profits. If there is a norm, it is probably around one-third of available profits or, put another way, three times covered.

The same applies to interest payments. The lender wishes to know how prudent and realistic the borrower is by testing the extent to which pre-interest profits are available to pay the interest costs. If the interest payments form too high a proportion of the pre-interest profits, he will know there is very little cushion to absorb profit reductions. And, because profits are a residue from the difference between two relatively high figures, ie income and expenses (quite possibly 100 and 95), it is relatively easy for the 'residue' to be rapidly squeezed. This is even more likely if the business is working on high fixed overhead costs. It is therefore important that there should be ample income cover to guard against unplanned setbacks, in the knowledge that interest payments can continue to be met without strain.

The same principle applies in relation to the level of borrowings and the assets which are available to secure them.

Standard covenants in borrowing agreements would usually include:

- interest cover (as referred to above)
- maintenance of tangible net worth (or a particular rate of growth)
- ratio of tangible net worth to total borrowings
- ratio of total liabilities to tangible net worth.

Example
Let us suppose that a company has two term loans as shown on page 58.

In this example, it can be concluded that there is generous earnings cover. It will be normal to examine the sensitivity of the profit to adverse changes in critical factors, particularly in respect of changes in turnover, gross margins and the significance of fixed costs.

Other types of finance

Although banking loans form the preponderance of business borrowings, other significant types of finance are:

- leasing
- factoring
- hire purchase
- sale and lease back
- bills of exchange
- documentary credits
- loan guarantee scheme
- export credit guarantees.

Leasing
A lease is a contract under which one person, the lessor, owns an asset

		Annual interest charge
	£	£
8% secured loan	250,000	20,000
10% unsecured loan	500,000	50,000
Capital and reserves	2,000,000	
Return on capital (before interest)	20%	
Intangible assets	200,000	
Tangible assets are therefore	1,800,000	

Capital cover

	£	£000	Tangible asset cover	Aggregated borrowings cover
Secured loan (priority)	250,000	$\dfrac{1,800}{250}$	7.2	
Unsecured loans	500,000	$\dfrac{1,550\star}{500}$	3.1	
Total borrowings	750,000	$\dfrac{1,800}{750}$		2.4

★ Calculated on net tangible assets less secured priority loan

Income cover

Profit pre interest £400,000
(20% on £2m)

	£		Income cover	Aggregated income cover
Secured loan interest	20,000	$\dfrac{400}{20}$	20	
Unsecured loan interest	50,000	$\dfrac{380\star}{50}$	7.6	
Total interest payments	70,000	$\dfrac{400}{70}$		5.7

★ Calculated on (400–20) = £380K

which is made available for use by another party, the lessee, in consideration for periodic rental payments.

Leases fall into two broad categories. The first is known as a *finance lease*. It is tantamount to complete ownership by the lessee. The lease covers the expected life of the asset. The lessor's investment and interest costs will be fully recovered through the rental payments, with the lessee responsible for all other costs, such as insurance and maintenance. At the end of the lease, the asset technically reverts to the ownership of the lessor, but there will be provision in the lease for extension at peppercorn rent or the right to buy outright for a negligible price. If the asset is sold to a third party, nearly all the proceeds of sale will be paid over to the lessee by way of rental rebates.

The second category is known as an *operating lease*. This may be for short or long periods, but is not structured in the manner of a finance lease because it is expected that the lessor will lease to other parties during the currency of the asset life. Normally such leases contain short notice termination provisions which are absent from finance leases. There are occasions when the right to terminate can be of some embarrassment to the lessor, as was the case, for example, with certain computer leases where the equipment was effectively obsolescent owing to changing technology, thus rendering re-leasing virtually impossible.

It can be expected that changes in tax law will adversely affect the price of leasing. When capital expenditure ranked as a 100 per cent tax allowance, part of the benefit would frequently be reflected in the rental charge. Since 1984, this benefit has been reduced and, under current legislation, the only tax benefit attaching to the asset acquisition is the annual writing down allowance (save for certain specified geographical areas designated for preferential treatment).

The advantages of leasing as against loans may therefore be considered marginal. The principal advantage may be through the smoothing of cash flows over a period of years and, in some cases, lower rental payments in the earlier years.

The fact remains, however, that many companies regard leasing as holding a proper and substantial place in the overall financial package although it is no longer acceptable to treat assets that are the subject of a finance lease as an off-balance-sheet item. A finance lease should be recorded in the balance sheet as an asset offset by an obligation to pay future rentals. For motor vehicles, there is a trend towards the use of operating leases.

Fleet contract hire
Although not strictly a borrowing matter, it is perhaps appropriate to

refer here to fleet contract hiring, which has other operational advantages. With the complexity of road transport vehicles and company car fleets there is increasing emphasis on more sophisticated transport management. It is not sufficient to consider only vehicle acquisition, although the options there deserve proper analysis – cash purchase, leasing and hire purchase being three of them.

Ownership of the vehicles is not itself particularly important. The key consideration is the effective cost of operating the transport fleet, which embraces acquisition, repairs and maintenance, running costs and disposal. The total fleet cost is a significant element in company expense. Large numbers of employees receive part of their compensation package in the form of a car, with a further number of senior managers now having the use of a second company car. Personal choice of car makes it also more acceptable. And so there is a growing need to seek greater efficiency in fleet operation, more control over mileage use and greater need for accident-free operation.

A developing option, therefore, is the use of an operating lease (as opposed to a finance lease) otherwise known as *contract hire*. There are other related benefits because a fleet under contract hire is still treated as an off-balance-sheet item.

The following factors are relevant:

- The difficulty for relatively small fleet users to provide a cost-efficient, in-house transport management service.
- The need for sophisticated computer analysis if fleet costs are to be properly analysed and results presented in a form easily usable by management.
- The advantage of large contract hire companies being able to provide a professional service backed by sophisticated computer applications from which operating efficiencies may flow. In such circumstances, the apparent increase in charges payable to the contract hirer may be more than offset by consequential fleet effectiveness.

Contract hire can cover a wide range of options, but may extend to a total service comprising, in addition of course to the vehicle itself (and here there are growing opportunities for efficient bulk purchase arrangements arising from increasing competition between car manufacturers), the following:

- servicing
- maintenance
- spare parts

- replacement vehicles
- accident repairs
- fuel
- insurance
- accounting
- management information.

Whether or not fuel cards are part of the contract hire, they are now providing useful fleet operating information. They may be issued by either petrol companies or independent operators. Specialised computer applications in this area can provide management with detailed analyses and improved car usage control.

Factoring

The essence of factoring is the sale or assignment of trade debtors to a finance house, the consequence of which is to release cash to the company within a short time of effecting the credit sale. The finance house may well be a bank, as most banks now provide a specialist service of this nature.

The arrangement with the factor may provide for him taking full risk of debt collection known as non-recourse factoring. Or the factor may have the right to disclaim the credit risk with recourse to the seller in the event of non-collection of the debt.

The debt assignment may be overt, with the consequence that the customer will be aware of the arrangement, or invoicing and other procedures may be carried out by the seller so that there is no third-party knowledge of the arrangement.

It is usual for the factor to be able to offer an accounting and credit control function as an additional service, for which there will be a fee which usually works out between 1 and 2 per cent of invoiced sales.

It is also usual for a substantial payment to be made by the factor on transfer of the debts, perhaps of the order of 80 per cent, with the balance, less factor's fees and costs, to be paid over when collected, or at a previously agreed time after invoice date if the factor undertakes the full collection responsibility on a time-related basis.

The charge for the factoring service will usually approximate to a normal interest charge calculated on the amount and period of credit at an interest rate related to bank base rate.

As already mentioned, the pressure on cash flow can be severe for a rapidly growing business, with working capital demands increasing at a fairly consistent rate in relation to increases in turnover. Factoring provides an effective method of diminishing the pressures.

Such a service may be of special interest to companies which have international trading involving the granting of credit. In such cases, there are considerable advantages in using a factor or his overseas commercial agent to check out credit ratings and deal with invoicing or collections in the customer's language.

The cost of UK and international factoring is worth serious consideration. Smaller companies in particular, which cannot easily build up economic in-house departments, will frequently find the cost relatively moderate and more than competitive with internal costs if all the services and time involved are properly costed.

Hire purchase

A contract is a hire purchase transaction if one party, the hirer, agrees to pay another party, the owner, a series of payments during the period of the contract, with the hirer having the right to acquire title or ownership at the end of the contract by the payment of a nominal sum or automatically on payment of the last instalment. The essence of such an agreement is that title remains with the owner until the contract is satisfactorily completed, thus providing some protection against default by the hirer because of the right (subject to some quite extensive legislation) to repossess the goods which are the subject of the agreement. The instalment payments are a combination of interest and principal.

A *credit sale transaction* has many similarities to a hire purchase agreement. The essential difference, however, is that ownership passes at the time of the credit sale transaction. In the event of default by the purchaser, the vendor must rely on legal processes to sue for the unpaid debt and has no claim on the property itself.

Sale and lease back

Although not a borrowing in the accepted sense, selling a freehold property and simultaneously leasing it back is a fundraising transaction, substituting a future stream of rental payments for an asset which previously involved no cash outgoings.

For trading businesses there is considerable logic in so arranging property matters because a trading business is not essentially in the property-owning business. It requires security of tenure for the conduct of its operations which can equally well be arranged by leasing. Under normal circumstances a trading business ought to be able to make better use of its cash resources than having them tied up in secure but relatively low yielding fixed assets.

There are some restrictive aspects of leasing property, denying on occasions the ability to be flexible and to be able to rearrange matters without interference. Nevertheless, the need to own freehold property should always be carefully examined.

Bills of exchange

Bills of exchange have historically played a significant part in the conduct of international business.

A bill of exchange is defined in the relevant legislation (the Bills of Exchange Act 1882) as 'an unconditional order in writing, addressed by one person to another, requiring the person to whom it is addressed to pay on demand, or at a fixed and certain future date, a sum certain in money to, or to the order of, a specified person or bearer'. That is a very explicit definition. It will be seen, of course, that a cheque is, in fact, a specialised form of a bill of exchange. A bill arising from trade is known as 'a trade bill'.

By this method an exporter can draw a bill of exchange on an importer with the advantage that the parties do not necessarily need to know too much about each other in order to conduct international business. The advantages are twofold: the importer who signs (ie accepts) the bill obtains a period of credit in accordance with the terms of the bill, and the exporter can get access to cash by discounting the bill at his bank, at the cost of an interest rate for the period of credit. In due course, the bank presents the accepted bill to the importer for payment.

There is clearly some credit risk attached to the creditworthiness of the importer, but dishonouring a bill of exchange gives rise to a second course of action relating to the bill itself, quite separate from the unpaid debt. There is, therefore, a contingent liability attaching to the exporter, because the discounting bank will have a right of recourse against the drawer for non-payment by his customer. In an international transaction, the importer can be expected to draw the bill on itself and have it accepted by its own bank prior to the bill being sent to the exporter for discounting at its own bank. This is known in international terms as 'avalising' a bill.

A bill of exchange is a negotiable instrument. Therefore it can be traded in the financial markets by endorsement, dependent among other things on the financial quality of the various parties to the transactions. Until maturity of the bill, the acceptor has a liability amounting to its face value, and it will appear in the balance sheet as a short-term liability under the description 'bills of exchange payable'.

63

Documentary credits

There is a large variety of methods for ensuring payment by overseas buyers to the international trader. One of the most usual is that of the documentary letter of credit.

The letter of credit will be issued by a bank in the importer's country and either advised or confirmed by a bank in the UK. Only if it is confirmed by the UK bank does the UK bank have any obligation to pay or accept bills against the presentation of documents. Such a bill of exchange, when 'accepted' by the UK bank, can be readily discounted at fine rates in the London money markets, thus releasing rapid payment to the exporter at modest cost. There are both 'usance' letters of credit where bills are accepted against presentation of documents and 'sight' letters of credit where payment is made against documents.

The procedures are relatively complex and require in particular correct documentation.

Loan guarantee scheme

The loan guarantee scheme was introduced by the government in 1981 and is planned to last until at least March 1989. The purpose of the scheme is to assist in financing small businesses which cannot raise all or any of the funds they need. Often this will be a start-up situation, but not necessarily so. It will always be high risk, probably in circumstances where a business cannot raise enough capital for itself. The principle is that the government will stand behind the loan in cases where a bank is unwilling to make a loan because it would not satisfy all of the bank's normal lending criteria. But the lending bank has a responsibility to satisfy itself as to the general validity of the proposal.

The principal conditions relating to loan guarantee arrangements, which are now administered by the Department of Employment, are:

- Seventy per cent of any approved loan is guaranteed by the government. The borrower pays to the government a quarterly premium, now at the rate of 2½ per cent, based on the amount guaranteed.
- Only small businesses are eligible, but there are certain exclusions, for example, agriculture.
- Loans can be for the purchase of assets or for working capital. The purchase of shares in a company is not an eligible purpose.
- Maximum loan is £75,000.
- Loans are likely to be for terms between two and seven years. Principal capital repayments may be deferred for an initial period.
- All available assets will be the subject of a charge in favour of the lender.

It will be recognised that loans made under these arrangements are likely to raise the ratio of borrowing to equity capital to a higher point than would normally be regarded as prudent.

Export Credits Guarantee Department (ECGD)
Within the Department of Trade and Industry the ECGD is responsible for providing insurance to the UK exporter against the risks of selling in overseas markets. Its strategic purpose is to encourage the UK export trade.

The essence of the risk lies in the overseas buyer's creditworthiness. Because of strong international competition, often encouraged by national subsidy in one form or another, exporters often find it necessary to offer generous credit terms to overseas buyers to maintain competitive terms.

The UK government guarantee may principally be given in one or two forms: either to the exporter's bank, which provides finance to cover the credit terms arranged with the buyer, or to the UK bank which provides the finance directly to the overseas buyer. Normally, the maximum term guaranteed will not exceed two years, but exceptionally there can be longer periods (eg in the case of capital goods).

Sources of borrowing

	Characteristics	*Function*
1. Clearing banks	Branch network throughout UK and international operations	Any type of lending transaction.
2. UK branches or subsidiaries of foreign banks	Substantially London-based.	Any type of lending transaction.
3. Merchant and investment banks	Substantially London-based but with some regional representation (one has a branch banking network). Wholesale bankers.	Most types of lending with emphasis on larger customers and specialist services.

	Characteristics	*Function*
4. Export Credits Guarantee Department (ECGD)	The government guarantees approved foreign debts, thus reducing export risks.	Credit insurance.
5. Council for Small Industries in Rural Areas (CoSIRA), an agent of the Development Commission	Assistance to businesses in rural areas of England or country towns with less than 10,000 population, employing not more than 20 skilled workers in manufacturing or service industries. Note. Comparable arrangements exist in Wales and Scotland via the Development Agencies, and in Northern Ireland by the Local Enterprise Development Unit.	Loans, supported by experienced advice from business managers.
6. Leasing (Equipment Leasing Association)	Most banks and specialised leasing organisations.	Provide finance through equipment leasing arrangements.
7. Debt factoring (Association of British Factors)	Assignment of book debts to specialist finance companies or banks against commission. Most factoring is on a non-recourse basis.	Advances normally as a percentage of the book debt.
8. Finance houses (42 are members of the Finance Houses Association)	Companies associated with banks and independent specialists.	Specially concerned with the provision of instalment credit.

Company balance sheets

The Companies Act 1985 sets out the manner in which company liabilities are to be reported in the annual accounts. There is significant divison between those falling due within 12 months and those of a longer period. Borrowings which are secured must also be identified.

The classifications are:

- debenture loans
- bank loans and overdrafts
- trade creditors
- bills of exchange payable
- payments received on account
- amounts owed to group companies
- amounts owed to related companies
- other creditors, including taxation and social security
- accruals and deferred income

Although the company has no legal obligation, until approved in a general meeting, to pay amounts recommended by the directors by way of dividend, under Section 235, it is usual to show proposed dividends under the creditors classification.

Provisions for liabilities and charges, for any liability or loss which is either likely or certain to be incurred but uncertain as to the amount or date on which it will arise, will be shown under this heading.

Although not a creditor in liability terms, reference should be made to contingent liabilities which must be covered in the notes to the accounts. These will include, for example, the existence of legal actions carrying potential liability, guarantees to third parties, bills of exchange discounted (because there are rights of recourse under certain circumstances), and goods sold under warranty. It is, of course, possible for contingent liabilities to become actual liabilities with adverse consequences for the company.

The following points are worth making in relation to the different categories of creditors listed above:

- The impact of liabilities falling due in the forthcoming period of 12 months may be significant and should be considered in relation to corresponding asset cover.
- In an insolvency situation, secured creditors rank ahead of unsecured creditors to the extent of their security. Where the security extends to a floating charge, it effectively means there are no assets available to other creditors (except to the holder of a fixed charge)

until the secured creditor is repaid. It is normal for banks to protect themselves in that way if they are able to impose their wishes on the borrower. Such pressure should, whenever possible, be resisted.

- These priorities between creditors therefore become important in the case of a winding up of the company or on the appointment of an 'administrator' by the courts by petition of unsecured creditors. Amounts secured by a fixed charge rank ahead of preferential debts.

There are two other potential difficulties. The first relates to purchases where, under the sale agreement, the title to the goods does not pass until the creditor is paid. This reservation of title is intended by the vendor to provide protection against other creditors. The second is a more remote contingency: under certain conditions government grants (for example, in respect of technology development) made to the company can become repayable in priority to other creditors.

Conclusion

Ensuring that all the financial arrangements are appropriate to the business requirements requires skill and good judgement. It is usually advisable for companies to seek professional advice, the total package being as much an art as a science. The consistent principle, however, is the proper matching of funding sources against the different types of asset required in any business activity and the maintenance of prudent ratios of borrowing to capital.

The cost of borrowing in its diverse forms is represented by the interest charge which is influenced by several factors including national and international interest rates, and the creditworthiness of the borrower, the nature of the business being conducted, the availability of security and the term of the loans, all of which will determine the margin payable by the borrower over the relevant interest rate.

A key factor in banking judgement is the perceived quality of the board and management of the company. Confidence on the part of the lender is of the utmost importance.

Chapter 4
Capital

The incorporated company

The second of the two basic forms of business funding is capital. While quite different in nature from borrowings, the two are closely related. But the key element is the capital base of the business. Without it, there is no basis for borrowing, which can range from no borrowings at all to a level approaching 100 per cent of capital. It is normal for capital to form the majority of the total business funding, say in the range of 60 to 70 per cent, with borrowings forming some 40 to 30 per cent. If borrowings become entrenched at a higher proportion than that, consideration should be given to increasing the capital base to bring the relationship to a more prudent ratio.

The concept of the joint stock company first became legally recognised in the UK in 1844, followed by the limitation of liability in 1855 and, in 1862, the first of a series of Companies Acts. It was a necessary development to satisfy the growing demands for business capital required by rapid industrialisation, as individual proprietors could no longer meet the growing capital needs from their own resources. To encourage the provision of capital from a wide range of individuals required the creation of a corporate vehicle which recognised the provision of capital by investors as the shareholders in the company and the appointment of directors and managers on their behalf to manage the business and account for their stewardship from time to time.

With this also came the concept of limited liability, for a wide range of investors not in close touch with daily activities would be unlikely to be attracted if they had no control over future, unknown demands on them. To admit limited liability therefore required regulation of a company's affairs for the protection of those who provided credit to the limited liability vehicle. This triangular relationship – shareholders, directors and creditors – has since been the fundamental concern of legislators in the development of corporate law to meet the changing business requirements. The latest relevant company legislation is the 1985 Companies Act, an extensive consolidating Act. In parallel with the growing complexity of business there has emerged a vast amount of legislation, much of which relates to public protection but always impacts the incorporated company.

Corporate legislation embraces the following key elements:

- The constitutional framework:
  - the Memorandum of Association, establishing the purposes of the company, and its capital formation;
  - the Articles of Association, establishing the internal regulations for the conduct of the company and in particular the rights of the members (shareholders) and the powers and duties of the directors.

  These documents establish two fundamental principles. First, that the company is a legal person, quite separate and distinct from its shareholders. Second, that, when recognised by a Certificate of Incorporation, the two constitutional documents form a legal contract between the company and each of its members for the time being, thus binding them both in relation to the company and to every other member.
- The registration of all important company documents with the Registrar of Companies. The files are available for public inspection.
- The maintenance of specified statutory records including a share register, a register of directors and their interests, and particulars of mortgages and charges.
- Reporting to shareholders specified information on an annual basis, including profits and losses, a balance sheet, cash flows and a report by the directors. Where appropriate, on a group basis.

The development of the limited liability company and widely held share ownership leads naturally to the need for an easy method of transferring shares from one person to another. The Stock Exchanges satisfied that need for publicly quoted companies. The London Stock Exchange in particular has established its own procedures and standards relating to its members who comprise the share market as agents for those wishing to buy or sell shares. The savings of individuals and institutions can, therefore, be marshalled and channelled into companies through the issue of securities via the Stock Exchange. It is thus a mechanism for matching available savings with the capital demands of growing businesses, and so effectively directs scarce resources towards the most efficient users. A modern capitalist system cannot function satisfactorily without such a mechanism. An international capital market is rapidly emerging.

Share capital

The Memorandum of Association defines the authorised share capital and the nominal value of the shares of the company. The Companies Act 1985 and the Articles of Association govern the procedures to be followed for subsequently altering the share capital.

The following points should be noted:

- The authorised share capital fixes the maximum which may be issued by the directors.
- There may not be issued any form of securities which carry the right to conversion into shares if the full exercising of these rights would cause the authorised share capital to be exceeded.
- The share capital may comprise shares of different classes and each may have a different nominal value.
- Share capital may be issued as fully paid or it may be called up in stages. The aggregate amount of the calls made, together with any share capital paid up, represents the 'called-up share capital'.
- A partly paid share imposes an obligation on the holder to pay up the unpaid portion when further calls are made in accordance with the Articles.
- Share capital may not be issued at a price less than its nominal value, ie at a discount.
- Shares may be issued at a price in excess of their nominal value. The excess is called a share premium and is in effect treated as an integral part of the share capital. The 1985 Companies Act specifies the purpose to which the share premium may be applied.
- A share is allotted to a person when he acquires the unconditional right to be included in the company's register of members.
- Shares may be issued for a consideration other than cash.
- A company may issue redeemable shares. If so, the redemption conditions must be stated in the accounts.

Types of share capital

The capital of a company may consist of different classes of share, carrying varying degrees of risk.

The principal types, in order of increasing risk, are:

- preference shares
- ordinary shares
- deferred shares
- warrants to subscribe for shares.

Dividends are the rewards for investment in shares. They represent a distribution of profits and are paid net out of the surplus remaining after the charge for tax on net profits. This means that dividends can rise or fall dependent upon the success of the company, although it is permissible to pay dividends from reserves built up from undistributed profits from previous years. A prudent company will not distribute to its shareholders all the available profits because this denies the company the resources required for expansion and development, a large proportion of which derives from profits retained within the company. It is normal to expect dividends to be covered about three times or, in other words, only about one-third of available annual profits will be distributed. Nevertheless, it is expected that a company will grow and increase the amount paid out each year by way of dividend. The expectation of an increasing flow of dividends is a significant factor in the stock market price of quoted companies.

Preference shares

The characteristics of a preference share are that in a winding up it carries preferential right over all other types of capital and entitles the holder to a dividend, usually at a fixed rate, payable in preference to dividends on other types of share. Within the category of preference share there can be a number of variations:

Cumulative

If, for any reason, a company cannot pay its annual preference dividend, there can be none on other types of shares; and the arrears of preferential dividend will have to be paid from distributable profits before any other dividends can be paid. The Articles of Association usually provide that, in the event of failure to pay a preferential dividend, preference shareholders acquire certain rights, including the right to vote at general meetings. Normally they cannot do so. This is an important latent power which could affect the voting control of the company.

Redeemable

Preference shares are repayable by the company at a stated time or within a stated period at the option of the company. Normally this will be at nominal value, but it need not necessarily be so.

There are statutory provisions affecting the source of funds from which redeemable shares can be paid, namely either from the proceeds of a new issue of shares or from accumulated reserves. If the repayment is funded from internal resources an amount must be set aside from distributable reserves to a redemption reserve account corresponding in amount to the nominal value of the redeemed shares.

Participating
In some cases preference shares are entitled to a dividend in addition to the fixed dividend, depending upon the profits of the company. Usually this will be related to the rate of payment of the dividend on the ordinary shares.

Convertible
Convertible preference shares have the option to be converted into ordinary shares at a predetermined rate within a stated period.

A share with all these characteristics will therefore be described as 'x per cent cumulative convertible redeemable participating preference share'.

An issue of preference shares is appropriate where an investor may be seeking some preferential security compared with other investors. As a consequence of this, the fixed rate of dividend will be relatively modest. However, as can be seen from the number of variations which can attach to preference shares, it is quite usual for the preference shareholder to seek additional benefits dependent upon the success of the company. A preference share may be particularly appropriate in the case of business start-ups or young developing companies because:

- The financier obtains a preferential position in a high-risk situation.
- The financier can benefit from success through further participation in dividends and/or conversion into ordinary shares.
- The funding ranks as capital, which is beneficial in some circumstances as compared with loan finance (which may be secured and carries higher risk to the company in the event of inability to pay an interest instalment) and may improve funding ratios.
- The return on preference shares is likely to be lower than on ordinary shares. The more capital that can be funded in preference terms, the greater the return on the ordinary shares.

Ordinary shares

Ordinary shares are entitled to all the profits of the company, after the payment of tax and preference share dividends. They are often referred to as 'the equity' in a business.

Ordinary shares control the company through the voting rights which attach to them, thus giving ordinary shareholders the important power to appoint and remove the directors. The residuary interest of the ordinary shareholders will therefore include:

- ordinary share capital
- share premium account
- revaluation reserve
- profit and loss account.

The 1985 Companies Act permits the redemption of ordinary shares, although it is not possible for all of the company's ordinary shares to be redeemed.

Some ordinary shares may be non-voting and, as such, have all the rights and obligations of voting shares save only for the vital issue of control. The purpose of such arrangements was to permit control of the company to remain in a limited number of hands, particularly family or family trusts, while enjoying the benefit of raising capital beyond the capability of the controlling shareholders. For companies quoted on the Stock Exchange the existence of non-voting shares is no longer welcome. Companies which already have non-voting shares are gradually enfranchising them.

Apart from the retention of profits (by not distributing them as dividends) the issue of ordinary shares is by far the most usual and appropriate manner of financing the majority of a company's capital requirements. Their subsequent value is closely linked with the stream of dividends to which ordinary shares are entitled and the expectation of trends in future dividend payments.

Ordinary shares are frequently offered to the shareholders of some other companies in exchange for their existing shares. They therefore provide a ready means of currency for an acquisitive company. A company with a high price/earnings ratio is therefore in an advantageous position to bid for the purchase of other companies whose shares may be reflecting less successful management or which are, for some other reason, at a relatively depressed price.

Deferred shares

Deferred shares are relatively unimportant and unusual. They may arise from a company reorganisation, for example, in order to introduce new capital where it is necessary to recognise that the original capital has effectively been lost. This can be recognised by converting the original ordinary shares into deferred shares which carry no votes, have their dividend claims deferred to ordinary dividends and rank on winding up behind the ordinary shares.

Warrants

A warrant gives the holder the right to be issued with shares of the issuing company at a stated price within a stated period. Warrants are normally created as an added attraction to an issue of loan stock, and may subsequently be detached from the loan stock and sold as an independent security for stock market trading.

Warrants can be a high risk and volatile investment because of the considerable leverage which arises from movements (up or down) in the share price against a fixed option price.

Rights issues

Any company wishing to increase its cash resources may do so through an offer of new shares at a fixed price. Whether the company is quoted on the Stock Exchange or not, it is normal to make the offer attractive by pricing the issue at a discount to the market price. If it is not a quoted company, a calculation of the share value must be made; the issue price might be somewhat lower. In either case shares may not be issued at a discount to their nominal value.

To protect existing shareholders, the 1985 Companies Act requires that, in the first instance, rights must be offered to existing shareholders in proportion to their existing holdings of the class of share affected. This is known as 'pre-emption'. The Articles of the company usually contain specific regulations as to how rights issues can be dealt with and what powers the directors have to ensure the required funds can be raised in the event that some or all existing shareholders decline to take up their rights.

If a company proceeds with a rights issue, consideration must be given to the effect this may have on other parties with claims against future issues of capital, eg option holders. Adjustments will be required and it is usual for the company auditors to be responsible for recommending the appropriate adjustments.

In the case of a publicly quoted company, the procedures for effecting a rights issue are complex and fairly expensive, involving the equivalent of prospectus information and the satisfaction of Stock Exchange requirements. In October 1987, the Stock Exchange issued guidelines concerning shareholders' pre-emptive rights. They are dealt with in greater detail in Chapter 6.

Purchase of own shares

Although not a method of funding – indeed the contrary – it is worth noting that the 1985 Companies Act permitted for the first time the right of a company to purchase its own shares, provided that it does not acquire all of them.

It is necessary for the company, in a general meeting, to give specific authority by special resolution for the purchase of its own shares or a general authority which must be exercised within 18 months of the passing of the resolution. A company may follow this procedure if it has surplus cash available and, in effect, considers it more in the shareholders' interest to return it to them than to retain it within the company. This action may well increase the value of the shares not redeemed.

Capitalisation structure

Can any general rules be established concerning the capitalisation of a company? There is room for differing views concerning what is prudent and the extent of acceptable risk, with the consequence that boards can properly take different attitudes towards the structure of capitalisation.

It has been established that the relationship of borrowed monies to capital and reserves is an important factor in the broad funding structure. Except in special situations, such as start-ups and some venture capital deals, it is a prudent rule to hold borrowings at a ratio not worse than borrowing to capital of 1:2.

The second important factor is the projected cash flow. If the business is expected to be profitable with strong cash flows, it is probably sensible to make provision for the repayment of some capital. This may be most conveniently arranged by the issue of redeemable preference shares, providing part of the capital base necessary at the time of issue but which will only be necessary for the next several years – say up to seven or so. Such an issue may also suit the financier who may have subscribed for both ordinary and preference shares but who does not wish all of his resources to be tied up on a permanent basis. Although ordinary shares can be redeemed, the issue of redeemable preference shares probably provides the more suitable vehicle.

Indeed, the finance may have been arranged to include loans, redeemable preference shares and ordinary shares, perhaps with the loans carrying conversion rights into ordinary shares. So the general intent may be to offer a package of inducements to the financier, protecting him through loans ranking in priority to share capital, but giving him the opportunity to participate in capital growth through a favourable conversion process. With strong cash flows the preference shares can be redeemed and the loans converted into new ordinary capital, opening the way for additional borrowings and yet maintaining prudent ratios.

Whether other inducements must be given will clearly depend on the relative strengths of the company and its financiers. As has been established, participation of preference shares in profits may have to be conceded. If so, it will necessarily be to the detriment of the ordinary shares.

The thrust of the financial arrangements will be to raise the necessary funds at the cheapest price and with as few constraints as possible on the conduct of the business. For this reason, charging the assets will be avoided as long as possible.

Equity valuation

Growth in the value of the equity or ordinary capital is the principal financial purpose of the company. This is brought about by progressively profitable business, thus fuelling the growth in dividends and profit retentions within the company, generating increasing capital resources and further increasing borrowing capacity.

Is a high equity value relevant to the funding of the business? The answer must be yes, particularly in the following circumstances:

- It permits the raising of additional capital through the issue of new shares at a favourable price.
- It provides a share exchange currency for the acquisition of the shares of other companies with lower price/earnings ratios at a favourable price. By this method, acquisitions may take place just for the purpose of getting hold of the cash resources of the target company – in effect a disguised rights issue. But much more likely, shares will be offered as a substitute for raising cash to buy a company required for trading purposes. If the vendor does not wish to keep the shares offered in exchange, it is often possible to arrange for these to be placed with some other party.
- It implies an efficient and profitable business, thus generating strong internal cash flows and the ability to finance itself from

internal resources.

- It implies a rapidly growing capital base, thus opening the way for additional borrowings on favourable terms.

What, then, are the factors which influence the value of the equity capital? They include:

- Profitable business. This is determined by two key ratios:

  Adequate net profit margins, expressed as the ratio:

$$\frac{\text{net profit}}{\text{turnover}}$$

What is an adequate ratio will depend upon the nature of the business and the competitive situation. It may be as low as 3 per cent or higher than 25 per cent.

Adequate net profit in relation to the amount of capital employed, expressed as the ratio:

$$\frac{\text{net profit}}{\text{capital employed}}$$

Strong management and control over the amount of capital employed is an important factor in achieving a satisfactory return on capital.

- The capital value of a business is related to the expected future stream of earnings (profits). So far as listed companies are concerned, that part of earnings distributed as dividends provides one important influence on share valuation. The dividend will be expressed as a yield on capital value. What is accepted as a satisfactory yield depends on many factors, but particularly the business sector and growth prospects. The norm, however, might be considered in the UK to fall in the area of 2 to 5 per cent. The prospects for future dividend growth will be an important factor, so that prospective yield will strongly influence current values.

  In the case of private companies, dividend policies and attitudes are far less significant.

- The dividend policy of a company is clearly relevant. Distributions may be 'full', ie most of the distributable profits are paid out in dividends; or prudent, in which case the distribution will probably be one-third, or less, of the distributable profits.

- Net profits are most often expressed in terms of 'earnings per share' (EPS). Unless otherwise qualified, this will refer to 'after-tax' earnings, but it must be established whether this calculation is made on the actual tax provided in the accounts or on the standard rates of tax. There can be a significant difference between the two calculations. The earnings per share calculation is:

$$\frac{\text{net after tax earnings}}{\text{number of ordinary shares in issue}}$$

and will be expressed in pence per share. Because the number of shares in issue may vary in the course of a year, it will be necessary to calculate the weighted average number of shares in issue during the year.

Earnings per share is probably the single most important measure of successful operation and equity reward, and therefore another strong influence on share prices. Again, prospective EPS is more relevant than past achievements.

- From the price at which listed shares are being traded a further important ratio can be calculated:

$$\frac{\text{share price in pence}}{\text{earnings per share in pence}}$$

This calculation shows the price/earnings (P/E) ratio.

It will be seen from examining a list of stock market prices that P/E ratios can range from 10 or less to as high as 40 or 50. Unless there is some special factor at work, such as a prospective or actual take-over bid, the ratio is almost always a reflection of the market perception of future earnings capacity. This concept is equally applicable to private companies.

- Another factor which must be taken into account is the prospective dilution of the issued share capital. This can come about through the exercise of options or conversion rights, for example. It is usual to take account of this probability by making the earnings per share calculation on the actual issued share capital and also on a 'fully diluted' basis, after taking account of the share capital as it will be when the options or conversion rights have been exercised.

It follows that the granting of rights to the issue of ordinary shares must always be given the most careful thought. The granting of such rights opens the way to substantial capital value and can clearly have an adverse effect on existing holders of the shares. The Articles of Association will almost certainly contain conditions affecting the powers of directors to issue options and, in the case of listed companies, the Stock Exchange and the financial institutions have their own rules to ensure fair treatment of the existing holders of shares with limits established on the ratio that options may represent to the issued capital.

Share options

The granting of the right to acquire shares at a fixed price at a future time is known as a share option. The holder is given the right to exercise the option over a stated number of shares within a stated period of time. The principal purpose of a share option is to provide incentives to management to perform more effectively in the interests of the company as a whole. Options are therefore most likely to be granted to the managers of the company rather than to all employees (for whom there are other more appropriate schemes).

The Finance Act 1984 introduced a sensible tax regime in respect of share options granted in accordance with the requirements of the Act, effectively making them income tax free and capital gains tax free until shares are actually sold, tax then being assessed on the difference between the sale price and the option price when exercised. Prior to 1984, the tax treatment of options was far less sympathetic and therefore had little practical effect on management motivation.

Because the issue of options dilutes the holdings of existing shareholders, the Articles of the company and, if the company is listed or intended to be listed, the rules of the Stock Exchange and the attitude of City institutions impose a limit on the extent to which such dilution is acceptable.

On occasions, options granted to management are linked to the future profit performance of the company. It is a fact, however, that the great majority of such schemes have not done so. Some of the investing institutions are now pressing companies to relate the granting of options to management performance.

Details of unexercised options will be included in the notes to the accounts, providing information as to:

- the number of options granted
- the option period
- the option price.

If the company is already listed, there is no difficulty in determining the market price of the company shares and, from that, the price at which options may be granted at that date. In the case of non-listed companies it is necessary for the company to arrive at an agreed share valuation with the Inland Revenue. Frequently the auditors will undertake that negotiation on behalf of the company.

Conversion rights

Rights to convert from preference shares or loan stock into ordinary shares are another source of equity dilution, a condition which will be conceded only in terms of 'no acceptable alternative'. And, of course, the equitable price at which conversion may be effected, probably some years before the event, is a difficult judgement to make.

Nevertheless, the convertible loan is a useful method of financing and, in the case of a listed company, is a financial instrument acceptable to the market. Because it is, in effect, deferred equity, a listed company will need shareholder approval to the instrument except when applied as part of a rights issue or as part of the consideration in an acquisition.

A convertible loan is more tax effective than a preference share because the running interest payments prior to conversion are chargeable against profits for corporation tax purposes.

It is not unusual for a financier to subscribe share capital and also advance loans. Such an arrangement can arise, for example, in order to ensure that management is able to acquire a reasonable proportion of share capital which would be far more difficult if all the funding were arranged as share capital. Or, all the loans may not be provided by the principal financier. Provided there is sufficient equity, it should normally be possible to raise some borrowings from a more appropriate lending source. Such an arrangement may better satisfy both parties, who have different objectives.

The arrangement also makes sense if it is anticipated that cash flows in the early years will be strong and likely to exceed what needs to be retained in the business. In such a case, putting up funding on a split basis is in the interests of all parties. Surplus cash can be applied to repay the loans, rather than accumulating it in the business. Moreover, the financier can particularly protect himself against failure of the company to achieve the expected levels of surplus cash by providing, in the agreements, that in such an event the financier has the right to convert some or all of the loan into ordinary shares. This is a fair provision since the management will only lose its position by dilution because of its own failure to achieve the planned cash flows it had held out when the funding was raised.

81

Sources of share capital

There is a wide range of opportunity to raise capital, or a combination of capital and loans, for business start-up and ongoing development. Nevertheless, in spite of far more active encouragement by the government in the last few years, it remains, in my experience, quite difficult to secure finance for new business ventures. This is particularly the case if the business is not dependent on assets – service businesses, for example, where much increased entrepreneurial activity has been generated. There are no short cuts. Several, sometimes many, financial sources have to be approached. Each has to be provided with a professional presentation (as explored in Chapter 2); discussions have to take place; quite probably the provision of further information involving detailed work in order to reach a decision.

This general procedure can take place on many occasions and can be frustrating and disappointing. The overriding needs are for determination and to allow far more time for the fundraising task than most entrepreneurs ever bargain for. It is, of course, easier if the promoter has some personal finance, for he will be asked on every occasion how much he will be risking. And yet many who deserve to succeed are short of that vital ingredient – personal capital. They will almost certainly have devoted months of their own time, possibly without any other income, to researching and developing the project. Professional accountants, lawyers, sometimes patent agents, will have been involved. Many of these people are today highly supportive of promising schemes and willing to devote time without fees until the project is launched.

In my experience, there is seldom anything so difficult in financial matters as obtaining adequate financing, within a reasonable time, for the so-called 'green field' operation, involving as it does unproven products or service business and untested management in that particular business activity. Many UK finance houses are not willing to undertake the risks involved and to devote the necessary management or board time to the project. But it is as well to be mentally equipped for the game which is only just starting; the early period of a new business can be likened to an obstacle race when, somehow or other, a new obstacle appears just when the course seems to be fairly under control!

It may be helpful to review briefly the protential sources of capital and some of their characteristics:

- The first source of funding a business is the internal generation of cash from the conduct of profitable business and the retention of resources within the business. This is maximised by management aiming to secure a high ratio of net profit to turnover and a high rate of profit return on capital resources tied up in the business and therefore increasing the rate of return. The effective use of capital can be measured by dividing the annual turnover by the average capital employed. The faster the rate of turn, the more effective the use of capital employed.

- Personal finance or finance subscribed by family, friends and acquaintances. Some resources of this nature will most probably need to be found by private companies because financiers want the promoter fully committed in every way. This is quite understandable because it is their real security. The promoter may well be expected to raise some finance against the security of his own house. I personally dislike the idea and have always tried to avoid that responsibility when involved in supporting new ventures. Because capital of this sort may be in short supply, and because most promoters want to control their own destiny by having more than 50 per cent of the voting capital, some ingenuity will be required in the structure of the financing to satisfy differing objectives. This may be done by giving the promoter substantial options for achieving predetermined targets, frequently referred to as milestones: preference capital to the financier, possibly with conversion rights and a dividend holiday for the first year or two, loans with conversion rights, are examples of seeking to reconcile the potentially competing interests of the parties involved.

- Finance subscribed by individuals as part of their personal portfolio spread. This source of capital, so much more readily available in North America than in the UK, and frequently so appropriate in the sense that there is often local knowledge and frequent contact between the parties, has in recent years been encouraged in the UK through the Business Expansion Scheme (BES). The prime factor is the granting of income tax relief to the individual who invests in projects which conform to some fairly stringent rules which have been amended and developed since the Finance Act 1983 first introduced the concept.

As a result of this legislation, the providers of finance and those seeking it have been brought together through the formation of a considerable number of BES funds whose purpose is to invest their clients' funds on an individual basis in those projects which the fund managers have examined and considered worthy of their financial support. And having thus decided to invest the fund manager will take an ongoing interest in the management of the business, with the intention that his investment shall be realised at a satisfactory (ie as defined by the fund management criteria) profit within the medium-term future (perhaps around five years or so).

Fund managers and venture capitalists usually aim to achieve a return on their investment taking into account capital appreciation and income flow, discounting the future expectations to present value to show a return of the order of at least 30 per cent per annum.

The Business Expansion Scheme
Because of its growing importance in the funding of small- and medium-sized companies, it is worth reviewing the principal features of the scheme.

- The principal purpose of the scheme is to encourage new business activity and create new employment opportunities in the UK. For this reason, the rules require that the company shall be incorporated and resident in the UK and that its trade shall be mainly carried on in the UK. It is clearly permissible for the company to trade internationally provided this is not the principal part of the business during the five-year tax relief period. As international trade can take place in many different forms, care will be needed and advice taken as to the best method of conducting the company's business in international markets.

- The company must not be quoted on the Stock Exchange or dealt in on the Unlisted Securities Market. But the 'third' market may be used for fundraising. All its capital must be fully paid up and it must not be a subsidiary of, or controlled by, any other company.

  It must carry on a qualifying trade or exist to hold shares in qualifying subsidiaries. The company may have subsidiaries provided that, throughout the relevant period, they are at least 90 per cent owned and exist to carry on qualifying trades.

- Most trades qualify for the purposes of the scheme provided they are being conducted on a commercial basis and with a view to profit, but there are important exceptions. These include dealing in commodities and financial instruments; the provision of financial services; oil extraction activities; leasing and receiving royalties or fees; and providing legal and accounting services.

  A business will not qualify if, very broadly, the value of the company's land and buildings (after deducting certain related liabilities) exceeds one-half of the net value of the company's assets. There are special rules for companies engaged in film production, research and development, oil exploration and ship chartering.

- Income tax relief is available to individuals who are UK resident and are not connected with the company throughout the five-year relief period; in particular the investor must not be an employee, partner or paid director and he (and his associates) must not control the company or own more than 30 per cent of the ordinary share capital or voting power.
- Tax relief can only be claimed by a qualifying individual subscribing for new eligible shares of a qualifying unquoted company for the purpose of raising money for a qualifying trade which is being, or will be, carried on within two years.
- Tax relief cannot be claimed on more than £40,000 in any tax year and is not given for investments of less than £500 in any one company in any tax year where the claimant invests directly.

Relief will be lost if the company ceases to satisfy the qualifying conditions within three years of making the investment. Relief is also wholly or partly withdrawn if the claimant 'receives value' from the company or disposes of his shares within five years. 'Receiving value' would arise, for example, if the company redeems the shares or makes a loan to the claimant.

Relief is available during the tax year in which the shares are issued, provided that the main purpose of the investment is not part of a scheme aimed at tax avoidance.

Capital gains tax will not be payable on chargeable gains (nor, therefore, will losses be relieved).

Appendix 4 sets out the rules in greater detail, but because of their complexity it will be sensible to seek professional advice in appropriate cases. The following illustrates the application of the scheme:

	BES investment £	Non-BES investment £
Cost of investment	5,000	5,000
Less: tax relief (say 50% tax rate)	2,500	–
Net cost of investment	2,500	5,000
Gross disposal proceeds	12,500	12,500
Capital gains tax (say 30% tax rate)	–	(2,500)
Net disposal proceeds	12,500	10,000
Profit on net cost of investment	10,000	5,000
Percentage increase	400%	100%
Approximate compound annual return at year 5	40%	19%

- Industrial companies. This source should always be considered but, unless the industrial company has, as a matter of policy, set up its own venture fund, it will be most likely to invest in projects which have synergy with its own business activities and with the intent that they will wholly control the new business in due course, and probably from the beginning.
- Venture capitalists. There is a substantial UK venture capital market. Those engaged in the activity may be 'stand alone' venture capital companies or an integral part of a UK clearing bank or foreign bank established in the UK. Such activities are also pursued by pension funds and some life assurance companies. The merchant banks also engage in this business. Some or all of these parties may work together as syndicates, with one acting as leader in the financial investigations and in bringing the project to an operational state.

  As has already been said, however, all of these funds are happier working to provide development capital, with the target business established and profitable and with some sort of track record. Very substantial sums can be raised for good business prospects. Seeking satisfactory financial support for 'green field' projects is much more difficult.

  Investors in Industry (3i), owned by the clearing banks, should be mentioned as the most significant investor in the UK venture capital field. Attention should also be drawn to the possibility of raising finance from one of the many USA-based venture funds, particularly if substantial US business is planned.

- Funds primarily established to provide employment in areas of declining industry. The British Steel Corporation and British Coal have both set up funds which are intended to assist job creation on a commercial basis in areas which have been badly affected by redundancies arising from the reorganisation and rationalisation of declining industries. BSC has been particularly active. Comparable financial support has been provided by some industrial companies in similar circumstances. Pilkington Bros plc is one example.

- British Technology Group. A government agency whose primary concern is investment in technologically based business.

- Stockbrokers. Many stockbrokers offer advice to their clients concerning investment in a range of business activities including start-up, development finance and BES funds.

- Stock market. Access to capital for any substantial and growing business is most appropriately satisfied through a public offering.

Share placements can also most easily be considered in this category. Chapter 6 deals with this aspect of financing.

- Management buy-outs. A rapidly increasing trend in recent years has been the management buy-out. As the name implies, the management of a business offers to purchase the business from its present owners. Chapter 7 deals with this activity.

Conclusion

Professional skill and judgement are required to complement the most effective company capital structure with that of company borrowings. One alone should not be considered in isolation.

The investor's aims are for a future stream of increasing earnings and dividends, essential to underpin the base for the second investment requirement – increasing capital value. Perhaps the most effective single measure of economic performance is net profit related to issued share capital as reflected by the 'earnings per share'.

In the UK there is a very wide range of professional financial institutions whose purpose is to advise about these matters, to arrange the most appropriate corporate financial structure and to act as financing principals.

Chapter 5
Government Assistance

Introduction

There is a wide range of assistance from the government which is basically directed at either helping employment creation in certain geographical areas where there is considered to be a structural unemployment problem or assisting industry to make technological improvements, to develop new products, to make more efficient use of labour and to develop export markets.

The assistance available is spread throughout government departments. It is, therefore, quite difficult to know what is available and how it can be obtained.

With certain exceptions, it is essential to apply for grants before a project is commenced. Schemes are discretionary and whilst government departments want to help, proposals are carefully examined and assistance provided sufficient only to achieve desired government objectives.

The statutory authority for the majority of government assistance derives from:

- the Industrial Development Act 1982 (which incorporates the Industry Act 1972);
- the Science and Technology Act 1965.

An outline of the type of government assistance available is given below.

Geographical assistance

The principal assisted areas which are beneficiaries of support are, in order of priority:

- Special development areas (mostly centred on Glasgow, Newcastle and the North East, Liverpool, Cardiff and Northern Ireland).

- Development areas (mostly centred on the Highlands, South West Scotland, Cumbria, Humberside, South Wales, South West England).
- Intermediate areas.

Financial assistance in the form of Regional Development Grants (RDGs) is for new investment projects connected with manufacturing or certain specified services, and which create jobs. The rules affecting RDGs are well specified to remove as much uncertainty as possible. The grant will be made on the basis of 15 per cent of approved project cost relating to buildings, plant and machinery (but not land), but modified in some cases by the costs related to the number of jobs created.

In intermediate areas, financial assistance takes the form of Regional Selective Assistance which is granted on a discretionary basis provided that the claimant establishes that the assistance is necessary for the project to proceed, or would benefit the area in a way in which it would not in the absence of the grant (which in this case may include land).

The assisted areas also benefit from the provision of government-financed factories, mostly of standard units, which are particularly suitable for small and start-up businesses. Because they are built speculatively in advance, much time can be saved getting them operational.

In addition to the assisted areas, there is a National Selective Assistance Scheme whose purpose is to encourage investment projects which will yield significant economic benefits in the national interest. This assistance is available to any business anywhere, provided it involves investment in excess of £500,000 and where the claimant can, as a consequence, demonstrate benefits which would not otherwise materialise.

There are three other geographically related schemes. The first, under the Inner Urban Areas Act 1978, provides for assistance to projects in the inner cities. The legislation provides for loans or grants for a wide range of activities deemed helpful to encourage business development in inner city areas. There is also assistance through the Urban Development Grant to encourage partnership between private enterprise and local authorities in run-down urban areas, the public sector contribution being shared between the local authority and central government.

The second relates to designated Enterprise Zones, small areas intended to encourage new business by providing exemption from rates for a period of ten years, 100 per cent capital allowances on industrial buildings, and to reduce problems usually associated with the granting of planning consents.

The third relates to the designation of a limited number of areas as 'freeports'. They are therefore regarded as being outside the UK custom area, thus permitting an entrepôt trade to be developed without the bureaucratic formalities normally associated with the import and export of goods not intended for UK domestic use.

Enhanced industrial production

The assistance available can be reviewed under two broad headings. The first relates to the provision of consultancy services, and second to other types of direct grant, for innovation and research and development.

Consultancy services
- Manufacturing Advisory Service
  This scheme is operated by the Product Engineering Research Association (PERA) on behalf of the Department of Trade and Industry. It is available to help only manufacturers employing not fewer than 60 employees nor more than 1000.

  The assistance, intended to improve productivity, comprises 15 days of consultancy service provided by approved consultants without payment and a further 15 days which is eligible for grants up to 50 per cent.
- Other advisory services
  PERA administers a technical advisory service to counsel small firms on technical problems.

  The Design Council provides an advisory service in connection with the engineering implications of improved industrial design which is available on the same basis as MAS.

  A marketing advisory service to assist small- and medium-sized businesses is available under the auspices of the DTI.

  There are a considerable number of information and counselling centres established throughout the UK providing a local business information service and a further substantial number of enterprise agencies to offer advice to small businesses.

  Grants up to 25 per cent, with a maximum of £25,000, are available to improve quality control procedures in order to secure compliance with a relevant British Standard.

  Finally, businesses with fewer than 200 employees operating in specified areas which have been substantially reliant on textiles, fishing, steel or shipbuilding activities are eligible for grants towards the cost of consultancy services (and towards capital investment) under the Business Improvement Services Scheme.

91

- To assist in the application of microelectronics in industry, the DTI will provide grants up to £3,000 for consultancy services to establish potential.

Innovation

- Computer-aided design, manufacture and testing
  Support in the form of grants for consultancy services and up to one-third of eligible costs to encourage the adoption of electronic applications in the engineering industry. Similar financial support is available to encourage engineering firms to invest in flexible manufacturing systems which will cost more than £200,000 to develop and install.
- Microprocessor applications
  Grants up to one-third are available towards the cost of applying microelectronics to production or process manufacturing.
- Microelectronics
  Grants up to one-third are available towards the cost of research, design, development and launching of new microelectronic products and up to a quarter for the capital investment for manufacturing them.
- Telecommunications
  Grants may be available to encourage the production of telecommunication products to conform with new British Standard Institution standards, provided application is made within six months of their approval.
- Fibre optics
  Grants up to one-third are available to encourage the development of new applications for fibre optics and opto-electronics.
- Software
  Grants up to one-third are available to encourage the development and marketing of innovative software products.
- Industrial robots
  Grants are available to support feasibility studies and up to one-third of capital investment required for the development and manufacture of robots and in their application in industry.

Research and development

- Grants up to one-third of eligible costs towards research or development costs for commercially marketable products.
- Grants up to 50 per cent (maximum £25,000) towards strategic studies in connection with bio-technology projects and grants for feasibility studies. Additionally, up to one-third towards bio-

technology research and development costs.
- Grants up to 25 per cent of costs in respect of a wide range of research and development costs related to manufacturing which are administered by the Research and Development Requirements Boards.

Export

- One-third of the costs of market research to develop export markets.
- The British Overseas Trade Board (BOTB) provides, from its offices throughout the UK, information covering a wide range of subjects related to the practice of exporting and market information related to individual territories. There is a subscription service to provide exporters with up-to-date market information. There is also a market advisory service focused on particular products or services and particular export markets.
- The BOTB provides financial support to help smaller and medium-sized companies open up or develop foreign markets. Proposals involving less than £40,000 of eligible costs are not considered, but support can be considerable – up to £150,000 for up to a five-year period.
- Attractive terms are available to encourage attendance at overseas trade fairs and are usually associated with several companies operating in the same industry to take space at exhibitions and trade fairs.

Export Credits Guarantee Department
This department of the DTI guarantees against credit risks of the UK exporter (see page 65).

Employment

- Training services specially tailored for employers to meet the specific requirements of employees are offered by the Skill Centre Training Agency (Manpower Services Commission).
- Grant support for courses in computer skills.
- In connection with the Youth Training Scheme, grants may be available to employers for engaging trainees under a training programme.
- Up to 50 per cent grant may be available from the DTI for schemes

which involve training, retraining or resettlement.

- Subsidies up to £15 a week per employee may be obtainable under the Youth Workers Scheme to encourage employers to engage young inexperienced people at wage rates which fairly reflect that shortcoming.
- A grant of £750 to encourage employers to split one full-time job into two part-time jobs of approximate equivalence.
- Subsidy and grants to encourage employers to develop projects which will provide work of benefit to local communities.
- Grants to encourage service industries to set up in, or move people to, the assisted areas.

Other subsidies

- Financial assistance is available towards the cost of surveys and feasibility studies intended to save energy and promote industrial efficiency through more economic use of coal.
- Financial assistance from the Ministry of Agriculture is available to support a variety of schemes with the general intent of improving farming efficiency and also to encourage forestry planning.
- Grants to encourage development of the fishing industry.
- Consultancy services and grants by the National Tourist Boards to encourage schemes intended to improve the attractiveness of the UK to foreign visitors.

Conclusion

This summary is intended to give some indication of the financial assistance available and most likely to be suitable for the smaller or medium-sized company.

There is a very wide range of consultancy and advisory services, subsidies, grants and loans aimed primarily at improving the competitiveness of UK industry and services, and to promote employment prospects, specifically in relation to the assisted areas.

Information about the government schemes is not readily available in any one place. Schemes are mostly operated by departments of state and specialised sections within each, but the Department of Trade and Industry library will be found helpful. The most comprehensive guide to the relevant information may be set out in a publication compiled by the Centre for the Study of Public Policy at the University of Strathclyde entitled *Industrial Aids in the UK*, first published in 1982 and subsequently renamed and revised as *Government Support for British Business*. There is a growing role for consultants familiar with the complex facilities available.

The availability of such a variety of government schemes can be of advantage to a wide range of businesses, and should always be considered in relation to funding requirements. It is, however, important to remember that the majority of the schemes have a discretionary element and that approval must be obtained prior to commencing any work or activity intended to benefit.

Chapter 6
Widening the Share Market

Introduction

So long as a company remains private, shareholders are in practice restricted in transferring their shares to third parties – there will almost always be restrictions in the Articles of Association, or in a shareholders' agreement, on the free transfer of shares. Normally, the vending shareholder has first to offer them to other shareholders and, because there is no open market in the shares, some artificial valuation method has to be adopted to determine the transfer price. Neither constraint is particularly satisfactory once a company becomes established and profitable; moreover, because of such restrictions it is most likely that the valuation will be discounted because of the absence of a satisfactory market. The opportunity to realise value by existing shareholders is, therefore, a powerful motive propelling the company to open up an exit route for the owners of the business.

A second reason, probably of about equal weight, is the need or opportunity for a company to introduce new capital or loan monies by a public offering which can be brought about by a number of different methods. All of them, however, are directed at opening the door to raise capital far more easily than is the case with tightly controlled shareholdings whose shareholders are frequently unwilling to continue to supply additional capital through rights issues. Company development and growth is almost always paralleled by the need for additional funding.

These are by far the two most powerful reasons for a company to seek a more responsive market and, even if the dominating motive is to provide shareholders with an exit route (which does not by itself raise funds for the company), the opportunity will automatically have been created to tap a wider capital market for the issue of new shares which will benefit the company resources through the injection of additional capital, or provide take-over 'currency'.

The public company

Only a public company may:

- offer shares or debentures to the public;
- allot such securities with a view to their being offered for sale to the public.

The Companies Act 1985 defines a public company as one whose Memorandum of Association states that the company is to be a public company and is registered as a public company under the provisions of the 1985 Act. In order to register as a public company, the essential requirements (which distinguish it from a private company) are as follows:

- The company name must end with the words 'public limited company' or with its abbreviation, plc.
- The Memorandum of Association must include a specific clause stating that the company is to be a public limited company.
- The nominal value of the allotted share capital must be not less than the authorised minimum. At present this amount is £50,000. Before the company can commence business or borrow money, a certificate of entitlement must be obtained and at least one quarter of the allotted share capital must be paid up. At present, therefore, this amount is £12,500. If there is a share premium, ie an amount payable per share in excess of nominal value, this amount must be fully paid up.

If a company is not registered as a public company, then it is a private company. It may be noted that this is a complete reversal of the requirements which obtained under the Companies Act 1948 where a private company was defined, and any companies not conforming to that definition were automatically 'public'.

The statutory regulations which apply to public companies are more stringent than those for private companies. A brief summary of the more important differences is set out in Appendix 5. For this reason, it is normal that a newly formed company will start life as a private limited company. In due course, in anticipation of seeking a market quotation, it will re-register as a plc, and amend its Memorandum and Articles of Association to conform with its more elevated status.

There may also be a commercial advantage attaching to a plc because of a perceived improved status deriving from its name as a public company, although in fact such a registered company need not seek public investment or stock market quotation.

Although some companies qualify early for full Stock Exchange listing, it may well be the natural progression to move first to the Unlisted Securities Market (USM) and, in due course, to seek enhanced market status by full listing on the Stock Exchange. Since inception of the USM in 1980, some 500 companies have been quoted, of which approximately 15 per cent have subsequently been granted full listing.

Public offerings

Before considering the methods by which share capital may be raised it may be helpful to set out briefly the current legislative position affecting public offerings. At the time of writing, the Financial Services Act 1986, Section 142 et seq, applies to companies which seek official (or full) listing on the London Stock Exchange.

In the case of companies seeking a quotation on other markets, for example, the Unlisted Securities Market (USM) and the Third Market, the requirements of the Companies Act 1985, section 56 et seq, still apply. However, the prospectus provisions of the Companies Act 1985 will be replaced when new rules as set out in the Financial Services Act 1986 are brought into effect at a date not yet announced by the Secretary of State for Industry.

Official listing on the Stock Exchange

The Council of the Stock Exchange has been appointed the competent authority for securities under the Financial Services Act 1986.

The Stock Exchange seeks to ensure that investors have confidence in the conduct of the securities market. To this end the Stock Exchange requires:

- that applicants for listing
  - are of a certain minimum size
  - have an adequate trading record under established management
  - set out in formal listing particulars sufficient information about the history, prospects and financial condition to form a reliable basis for market evaluation.
- that all transactions are conducted on a fair and open basis.
- that investors are treated with proper consideration by company boards.

The listing rules are briefly summarised in Appendix 6.

Only a member of the Stock Exchange can be responsible for sponsoring applicants for listing, and he deals with all relevant matters.

Notwithstanding that the directors of a company are responsible for the accuracy of the information set out in the listing particulars, and an issuing house may be acting as adviser to the company, the sponsor is held responsible by the Stock Exchange to satisfy himself that the company is in every way suitable for listing. Suitability for listing depends on all the relevant factors. Compliance with the listing particulars alone may not be sufficient. In this regard, the sponsor will pay particular attention to the composition, skills and experience of the board of directors, including non-executive directors.

The formal admission of securities to listing (and hence trading) is effected only when a notice has been posted on the trading floors of the Stock Exchange.

A condition of the listing is acceptance of 'continuing obligations' which apply after listing. They form the basis of the relationship between an issuer and the Stock Exchange. An outline of the nature of the obligations is set out on page 119.

Other listings

Securities offered to the public other than by way of an official listing will be by prospectus, which is presently subject to the requirements of the Companies Act 1985.

A prospectus is defined by Section 744, Companies Act 1985 as:
'Any prospectus, notice, circular, advertisement or other invitation offering to the public for subscription or purchase any shares or debentures of a company.' It is unlawful to issue any form of application for a company's shares or debentures unless the form is issued with a prospectus.

Section 56 (i) requires that the prospectus must comply with Part I of Schedule 3 to the Act and, if there is reference therein to any reports, the requirements of Part II must be complied with. It is unlawful and void to seek to avoid these requirements by obtaining a waiver from the offeree.

In an offer for sale (see below), the document prepared by the issuing house which has acquired the shares from a company for resale to the public must in every way conform with the prospectus requirements and, in addition, disclose the net consideration received by the company from the issuing house in respect of the shares which are the subject of the offer. These rules apply to offers made either within six months of taking allotment of the shares or at any time if the full consideration has not been paid to the company by the issuing house.

The prospectus requirements do not apply:

- to an underwriting agreement relating to the shares or debentures;
- to shares or debentures not offered to the public;
- to an offer by a company to issue its shares in exchange for the shares of another company (because the offer is not to the public in general or for subscription in cash);
- to offers deemed to be of personal interest between the offeror and offeree, eg directors inviting a number of their friends to invest in a company;
- to a 'rights' issue to existing members or debenture holders, even if renounceable in favour of third parties;
- to any document used to give information to individuals who may subscribe for shares to be issued as a private placement.

Before or at the time of issue a prospectus signed by every director and proposed directors must be filed with the Registrar and attached to it the consent by any expert or professional whose statement or report is contained in the prospectus.

The contents of a prospectus as required by the Companies Act 1985 are summarised in Appendix 6.

Methods

There are several methods by which wider share ownership through a public offering can be achieved. Briefly they are:

Offer for subscription
This is an offer to the public by a company of its securities intended for official listing by or on behalf of the issuer or following an offer for sale by an intermediary.

Offers for subscription normally apply to larger issues, for companies with market capitalisation of more than £10m and with pre-tax profits of more than £1m.

In the case of companies issuing equity shares for the first time, there is a limit of £15m at the market price, although there is no limit for companies already listed.

The Stock Exchange will need to be satisfied that arrangements will exist for an adequate market in the securities.

Offer for sale
This is a purchase by a financial house (for example, an issuing house, merchant bank or stockbroker) of company securities which may be either a new issue of shares and/or those of existing shareholders which

the finance house has undertaken to offer to the public.

Placing

This term describes the process by which securities are sold by a sponsor (for example, an issuing house or stockbroker) to selected buyers which may be financial institutions, private clients, employees or others invited to subscribe. The Stock Exchange requires that at least 25 per cent of the placed shares must be made available to the public in order to ensure an adequate market.

Placings are perhaps more appropriate for smaller issues through the Unlisted Securities Market and are less usual (but certainly not rare) in the case of the listed market.

The following is fairly typical of the way the directors hold themselves responsible for the information contained in the placing document applicable to full listing:

A copy of this document which comprises Listing Particulars relating to XYZ plc in accordance with the listing rules made under Section 152 of the Financial Services Act 1986 has been delivered to the Registrar of Companies in England and Wales for registration in accordance with Section 149 of that Act.

Application has been made to the Council of the Stock Exchange for the whole of the ordinary share capital of XYZ plc to be admitted to the Official List. It is expected that the ordinary shares will be so admitted with effect from 1 September 198– and that dealings in the whole of the issued ordinary share capital of the company will commence on 2 September 198–.

The Directors of XYZ plc, whose names appear on page [] accept responsibility for the information contained in this document. To the best of the knowledge and belief of the Directors (who have taken all reasonable care to ensure that such is the case), the information contained in this document is in accordance with the facts and does not omit anything likely to affect the import of such information.

If the registered office of the company was in Scotland, particulars would be delivered to the Registrar in Scotland.

It will also be normal to give key financial information in respect of the offer early in the document, along the lines indicated in the panel opposite.

The outline of the principal heads of a placing document is given in Appendix 7.

Placing statistics

Placing price	150p
Number of shares in issue	10 million
Market capitalisation at the placing price	£15 million
Percentage of share capital now being placed	25%
Earnings per share for the year ended 30 June 198- based on the current actual tax charge of 37.5%	10.0p
Price/earnings ratio at the placing price	15 times
Forecast dividends for the year ended 30 June 198-	
Net dividends per share	2.0p
Gross dividend yield	1.9%
Net tangible assets per share	35.0p

Note

For the bases and methods of calculation of the earnings per share, price/earnings ratio and dividend yield, see the paragraphs entitled price/earnings ratio and dividends, below (not shown).

Introduction

Where an adequate market (a matter of fact) in a company's securities already exists, securities may be introduced for the purpose of seeking a market quotation. Permission to do so must be sought from the Stock Exchange.

Subject to the restrictions in the Prevention of Fraud (Investments) Act 1958 and, when it is in force, the Financial Services Act 1986 (which will replace the 1958 Act), it may be possible to arrange private placings where securities are purchased by a restricted number of selected investors to whom shares are offered on the basis of financial information which is less comprehensive than with a statutory prospectus. No general market can exist for placings of this type.

Other methods of fundraising

Although different from the public offers described above, it is worth identifying other methods by which additional capital may be introduced.

Rights issue

A company can raise additional capital by inviting existing shareholders to subscribe for further shares. Under Section 89 of the Companies Act 1985 the new issue of shares for cash must be made pro rata to all existing shareholders on a pre-emption basis. This right can, however, be disapplied by a special resolution of the shareholders provided this does not take place more than 15 months prior to the issue, and many quoted companies seek such powers. As this can be prejudicial to shareholders, the Stock Exchange rules until October 1986 did not permit such action for quoted companies, but subsequent to Big Bang changed its policy by permitting new issues for cash, providing only that shareholders approved. Consequently, there could be a general disapplication, without any limits imposed by the Stock Exchange, by the authority of a resolution in general meeting.

Institutional shareholders have sought to protect their shareholding interests through Investment Protection Committees (IPCs) of the two representative bodies, namely the Association of British Insurers (ABI) and the National Association of Pension Funds (NAPF).

The attitudes of the two bodies differed in some respects, so the situation became confusing both to capital raising companies and to investors. Accordingly, new guidelines were issued by the Stock Exchange in October 1987, after agreement with both IPCs.

The IPCs hold the view that in principle the most appropriate course for companies wishing to raise additional equity capital is the offer of new shares to existing shareholders by way of a rights issue pro rata to existing shareholdings. And that, where issues take place on a non pre-emptive basis, there should be restrictions on the price discount at which the shares are issued. In the event of a 'combination issue' (comprising shares issued both on a pre-emptive basis to shareholders and an issue for cash to non-shareholders), the IPCs, while not opposing, regard them as exceptional and will monitor the situation carefully.

Provided companies conform with the guidelines relating to equity issues for cash other than on a pro-rata basis as summarised below, no further discussion with IPCs will be necessary. If, however, companies intend to exceed the guidelines, they are advised to seek early discussions.

- Listed companies should seek shareholders' approval annually by special resolution to disapply pre-emptive rights.
- The IPCs will advise their members to approve such a resolution provided that it restricts the annual disapplication to not more than 5 per cent of issued ordinary share capital.
- There is also a cumulative limit the effect of which is that, in any rolling three-year period, no more than 7½ per cent should be issued for cash on a non pre-emptive basis (the period normally starting from the commencement of the company current financial year).

- In the case of 'combination issues' there will be no opposition to the non pre-emptive element provided that it does not exceed 5 per cent of the issued ordinary share capital.
- In the case of non pre-emptive issues, shares should be priced at no greater discount than 5 per cent of the mid-market price immediately prior to the issue. Discount in this context includes fees payable to underwriters and sponsors. There will be no constraints on the issue of shares to existing shareholders at a greater discount.

Two disclosures are required:

- Immediately prior to and also following each issue discount information must be lodged with the International Stock Exchange.
- In the annual report and accounts companies should disclose details of the terms of issue during the accounting period, including net proceeds, the projected discount before issue and the actual 'opening discount' in the market.

As a general rule proposed issues which are outside the guidelines should be the subject of discussion with IPCs at the earliest practicable date.

Under Section 80 of the Companies Act 1985, directors no longer have untrammelled powers to issue shares (or rights to subscribe for shares or to convert securities into shares) whether for cash or a non-cash consideration. Directors must now obtain shareholder approval either by ordinary resolution which may not have validity for a period in excess of five years, or by the Articles of Association. It should be noted that the IPCs expect a general authority under Section 80 to be limited to one-third of the company's issued share capital.

Vendor consideration issue
If company securities are issued for the acquisition of a business or shares in a business, the effect is the same as the introduction of additional capital which is immediately applied for the acquisition of an asset. Such an issue dilutes existing shareholdings but, of course, not necessarily their value. The IPCs have indicated that they may protect their interests by claw-back arrangements if a substantial number of vendor shares are placed at a material discount to the market price.

Conversion rights
Rights to convert into shares from a loan to the company, from warrants attached to the loan, or through share options which are exercised have the effect of increasing the share capital and diluting existing shareholders. It is for this reason that the Stock Exchange and the financial

institutions impose limits on the number of share options which may be arranged, particularly those in favour of management. Further information is given on page 81.

Going public

There are four methods which can be followed in order to secure share marketability:

- Listing the securities on the principal Stock Exchange, known otherwise as a 'full' listing
  The requirements for seeking a listing are rigorous, and there are substantial, continuing obligations on the company thereafter, arising from the Financial Services Act 1986 and the requirements of the Stock Exchange in the interests of investor protection.
- A quotation on the Unlisted Securities Market (USM). Introduced in 1980 the unlisted market has provided an opportunity to achieve a regulated market in a company's securities, where the introductory requirements are less rigorous than for a full listing, and less expensive. It is particularly suitable for smaller, less mature companies, permitting founding shareholders a means of realising their investments, introducing additional capital to the company and currency for the acquisition of other companies. By the end of 1986 about 500 companies had taken advantage of the facility of which about 15 per cent have subsequently graduated to full listing and only about 3 per cent have failed for solvency reasons. It has therefore met a real need for the less mature company.
- Third market
  An additional share market, the third market, started trading early in 1987. It is designed by the Stock Exchange to encourage a market at very low entry cost. Key features of the new market are:

  - available for companies which qualify under the Business Expansion Scheme;
  - cheaper to enter and less regulated;
  - no criteria relating to minimum size (eg turnover or capitalisation);
  - no minimum percentage of shares need be made available for trading but the sponsors are required to ensure an adequate after-market;
  - the company must be a going concern with at least one year's audited accounts or it can be a start-up, provided there are

prospects for generating significant revenues within the first trading year;

- sponsors must ensure at least two market-makers for share dealing. (*Note*. A market-maker is an organisation which buys and sells shares as a principal. Before 'Big Bang' this function was performed by a jobber in the London Stock Exchange.)

It is expected that some companies now trading in the over-the-counter market (see below) will qualify for the third market. Responsibility for bringing suitable companies to the new market will lie almost entirely with the sponsor. It can therefore be assumed that he will adopt a cautious approach because his reputation will be right on the line.

- Over-the-counter market (OTC)
  This market, unlike the previous three, is not regulated by the Stock Exchange. Marketability is achieved by licensed dealers arranging for shares in a company to be offered to the public and making a market in the shares. It is less liquid than the more formalised markets but satisfies a need for companies in the early stages of their development, including in particular companies whose owners are able to secure tax relief under the rules of the Business Expansion Scheme.

- Reverse take-over
  One other method of achieving a listing should be mentioned. Under certain circumstances it is possible to arrange for an already publicly quoted company to issue its shares in exchange for the shares of a company to be acquired with the effect that the shareholders of that company emerge with the majority share-holding in the quoted company. Consequently, the acquired company becomes a wholly owned subsidiary of the listed company, and a public quotation has been achieved. This is known as a reverse take-over.

Pros and cons of a public quotation

The decision to 'go public' is extremely important and a turning point in a company's business life. For that reason it is not to be taken lightly. Public listing means that the board is exposed to external interest in a manner which cannot happen in a private company. Even so, there is a very limited number of companies which are publicly listed and yet still under family control: one of the methods of achieving this was for the founders to own a majority of the voting shares and for the public to subscribe for 'A' or non-voting shares which have precisely the same rights save only for the fundamental right to control the company. The practice of issuing non-voting shares is now unacceptable to the Stock Exchange and most companies who have enjoyed such a status in the past are moving towards enfranchising the deprived shareholders.

The advantages of public listing include:

- Opening up the opportunity to raise funds to increase share capital. Once listed, the avenue remains open for the future.
- Opening up the opportunity for shareholders to obtain a liquid market for some, or all, of their investment in the company. The issuing house will usually require an undertaking from substantial shareholders that they will accept restriction for a period on their ability to realise their investments once the initial sale on first going to the market has been agreed.
- Providing a currency for the acquisition of other businesses through the issue of shares by the acquiring company.
- Providing an opportunity for employees to convert share options into shares either under a SAYE or share option scheme.
- Providing the opportunity to facilitate the funding of the business by the issue of loan securities with warrants attached. The warrants are convertible into shares at the price stated when issued. Prior to conversion, warrants can be traded in the market, and usually have a very volatile price because of the gearing effect.
- Achieving a status which in some cases can be very important to the credibility of the company in its trading activities.
- Offering an opportunity to attract senior management to companies perceived to be playing in the big league and where option-related terms of engagement offer a significant benefit.

There are, however, some disadvantages which have to be accepted as a result of seeking public listing, as follows:

- The exposure of the company, which effectively means the board, to the scrutiny of a wide range of interested parties. In particular:
  - the media, occasionally radio and TV if there is some event of perceived wide public interest, but generally newspapers and specialist publications;
  - financial analysts, most of whom are employed by stockbrokers.

- The ability of predatory companies to purchase shares in the market and/or to seek to acquire control of the company by an offer to the target company's shareholders.

If the board does not control the shareholdings (which it seldom does) it will be a decision to be taken by individual or institutional shareholders in the light of all the perceived relevant facts, and if the members of the board do control the company, the personal interests of the individual director/shareholders may well diverge.

The offer may be a 'friendly' bid supported by the company board and recommended to the shareholders for acceptance or it may be contested.

City institutions and the Bank of England have sought to ensure fair rules in the interests of shareholders for take-over bids through a system of self-regulation by the Take-over Panel. The recent opening up of all City markets is likely to bring about more intense competition in every respect including company take-overs. It remains to be seen whether self-regulation can hold out against these growing pressures.

- The need to conduct the business in a more formalised manner and to ensure strict conformity with the rules of the Stock Exchange.
- The need to devote more time and energy to communicating with all the interested parties in the City and in particular to nurture support of the shareholding institutions which frequently hold the majority of the shares.
- The greater need to have a considered dividend policy and to try to reconcile the short term with the longer.
- To accept that pressure to improve financial results will be a fact of life, carrying more stress and the temptation to put short-term results before the business need for longer-term investment and development.

Requirements for a quotation

It is a serious decision to offer shares to the public. This is true whichever route is taken. Companies which seek quotation on the OTC market are not subject to the rules of the Stock Exchange but the directors have similar responsibilities. Investors know that in respect of these companies the risks are higher and the company less well established. For companies seeking a wider market, whether by way of a full listing or the Unlisted Securities Market, the strict rules of the Stock Exchange apply. The fundamental concern is the protection of the investors and this requires the business to have a competent board of directors, a properly financed company and growth potential.

All the professional advisers therefore give the most careful consideration to the quality of the offering and will take whatever steps they consider necessary to satisfy themselves that the offer is as fair as possible and that all relevant information is made available at the time. None of the care exercised by professional advisers in any way removes the fundamental and primary responsibility of the board for the disclosure of all relevant information and for the exercise of proper prudence in the preparation of information and in respect of profit forecasts which may be included in the prospectus.

The Companies Act 1985 and the Financial Services Act 1986 contain the statutory law relating to public offerings and the rules of the Stock Exchange reinforce and supplement the law. Both must be complied with.

Because seeking a quotation is complicated and must be approached with the greatest care, and because boards of directors must protect themselves from legal actions which can arise through misrepresentation or fraud, the board will take the greatest care in selecting its professional advisers upon whom it must rely to ensure precise conformity with legal and technical requirements.

Proper time must be allowed to consider the appointment of the most appropriate advisers. It is usual for the first step to be an approach to the sponsor who will carry prime responsibility for the task; and it is wise to make all the key professional selections at least six months before the planned offering. Because there is a wide choice of suitable sponsors, the chairman or a committee of the board will discuss the matter with a number of potential sponsors. This is not a one-way situation. During the discussions and interviews the sponsor will be considering carefully whether he is willing to risk his reputation in advising that particular company.

Assuming a mutually satisfactory selection is made, if the sponsor is not a stockbroker the board will consult with the issuing house and again go through a selection process to determine which broker is considered most appropriate for ensuring a satisfactory market situation for the company's shares once permission to list has been given by the Stock Exchange. Quite soon after that appointment has been made, and again in conjunction with the principal adviser, the board should proceed to select the most appropriate public relations agency.

These, and the firm of accountants appointed to investigate and report on the company affairs and, perhaps, the appointment of new legal advisers, are matters on which key decisions must be made. Obviously, sufficient time must be allowed at each stage. It is correct to assume that at least three months may be necessary to do the selection work properly, which means that the process must be started at least nine months prior to the offering date.

This will only be the beginning of a process which will require a great many hours of senior management time. The drain on management resources must never be underestimated, and one of the early board considerations will be how that burden is to be shouldered with minimum disruption to the running of the business over a period of more than six months. The professionals will provide a great deal of help in taking the company through unfamiliar territory, but the chairman, finance director and managing director must expect to devote a great deal of their time to the detailed issues leading up to the flotation.

Professional advisers

Sponsors
The role of the sponsor is to act as principal adviser to the company, to act as co-ordinator of the professional teams engaged in the work and to be responsible for the method, the timing and the pricing of the issue.

In the case of a full listing, it is likely that the sponsor will be a merchant bank or one of the specialist divisions in a clearing or foreign bank. But it could be a stockbroker, and in the case of the unlisted market, it is more likely to be. However, the banks add credibility to the marketing of the issue and offer a wider range of resources than the broker.

For full listing, the merchant banks in particular have established a strong position in the London market, built around highly professional corporate finance departments.

The enforced alteration of the trading terms of the stockbrokers, as from 27 October 1986, brought about a quiet revolution in the City, with, initially, the merging of brokers with bankers and the emergence of international, all-purpose finance houses. This is likely to have an effect on the traditional handling of share issues in the UK.

Stockbroker
If a stockbroker is not the sponsor, another broker will need to be appointed. His tasks are to ensure that all Stock Exchange procedural matters are complied with; to stimulate the interest of potential pur-chasers of the shares through other brokers, institutions and private clients; and to consult closely with and advise the sponsor concerning market conditions and his view as to the optimum price.

Before undertaking the task, in-depth discussions with the board and management of the company will almost certainly take place, and it is quite likely that the broker's analysts will be assigned to study the company business in order to obtain their own information and form their own opinions as to the suitability of the company for public offering.

Bank of England
To assist in orderly marketing, the Bank of England co-ordinates the dates reserved for bringing companies to the market. Normally it will be the task of the stockbroker to negotiate the date for his client, although occasionally it may be arranged at an earlier date by the merchant bank. It will be necessary to effect the reservation several months in advance.

Reporting accountants
A fundamental requirement of the sponsor is the appointment of reporting accountants to investigate thoroughly the affairs of the company and to prepare what is known as 'the long form report'. In order to prepare such a report, there will be a great deal of deep study and investigation into the state of the company, covering not only financial information but a whole range of commercial issues, including markets, products, internal organisation, management; and from these studies and information provided by management and board to form a view as to the company's prospects after the public offering.

Arising from this work, it may be necessary to rework or restate some of the financial information – for example, if some business activity has been closed down and will not be a part of the company business in the future.

The reporting accountants are also responsible for preparing the 'short form report', based on the longer version, which will form part of the prospectus.

A profit forecast may or may not be included in the prospectus. If the issue takes place reasonably soon after the company year end, there will be no necessity to include a forecast of the future profits. If, however, the issue takes place more than six months after the year end, it will be necessary for the directors to prepare a profit forecast. If so, the reporting accountants are required to examine the statement and to report on it.

Finally, the reporting accountants are required to report on the adequacy of the working capital requirement of the company after the issue.

The reporting accountants may or may not be the same as the company auditors. If they are, it will invariably be the rule that a different partner will be assigned to the investigation.

Lawyer

In addition to the company lawyers, the sponsor will almost invariably need to appoint a solicitor to advise on legal matters pertaining to the issue and the prospectus. If the company lawyers lack experience in issue matters, the board will need to consider the implications of that in their preliminary work concerning the appointment of professional advisers.

PR agency

It is becoming more usual to appoint a public relations agency to assist in the marketing arrangements. Specialist firms exist which are skilled particularly in City and financial affairs, and respected by the sponsors. It will be important for the board to ensure that there is full co-ordination between the PR agency and the company's own advertising and/or PR agency. It may be that the company advertising and promotional plans can be co-ordinated with the specialist issue requirements to 'add value' to the corporate marketing process.

Other advisers

Depending on the complexity of the business, other professional advisers may be required, such as property valuers, insurance brokers, pension and actuarial advisers. There is also a great deal of printing work to be done, much of it at short notice, and a skilled printer with issue experience will be required.

Finally, it may be necessary to appoint a company registrar, responsible for ensuring that all the necessary and detailed formalities are complied with. This is a substantial clerical load, where again skilled knowledge is available from the well-chosen professional company registrar.

Timetable

An indication of the timetable of the principal events which are likely to take place in the preparation for a public offering is set out in Appendix 8. Numerous detailed decisions and actions underlie many of the outlined principal events and the total programme is complex, parts of it critical. A director should assume control of the programme.

Considerations

When a company is considering a public offering, a large number of issues need to be addressed in order to ensure that the company is properly prepared for its changed role. Some matters needing attention are:

The board of directors
By far the most important issue is to ensure that the sponsor is satisfied that future investors will have confidence in the board's ability to run the company competently and to achieve its growth prospects.

Of the many factors the competence of the board as a whole and its integrity must be the overriding consideration. This includes the individual business reputation of the board members; the relative skills and expertise required to form a balanced team; the leadership of the chairman and managing director; the professional reputation of the financial director and the company secretary; and the breadth of experience brought to the board by two or three carefully selected non-executive directors. In some cases new appointments will need to be made in good time. This implies that such matters need to be reviewed at least a year ahead of the expected offering date. Because of its importance, the sponsor will most certainly take great interest in the board.

It is also desirable to avoid changes in the board after the offering. Assurances should be sought concerning the intention of individual directors to expect to continue in office for at least a year after the offering.

Finally, it will be sensible to consider the appointment of a senior director to be responsible for overall communications policy, both external and internal.

Company constitution
The Articles of Association of the company will almost certainly need to be rewritten in order to bring the regulations into line with modern practice and make them appropriate to a public company. This will, of course, require shareholder approval.

Contracts of service
The employment terms of executive board members and managers should be reviewed and contracts entered into to ensure, as far as possible, that there will be continuity of directors and managers vital to the business capability of the company.

Option schemes
With the opportunity to have a share quotation, thus permitting option holders to realise their rights, the company should consider its option

arrangements, particularly for senior managers and directors whose services should be more securely retained by the offer of tax-efficient share options. If the company has not already established a scheme under the Finance Act 1984, and it decides to do so, sufficient lead time must be allowed to prepare a suitable scheme and to obtain approval for it from the Inland Revenue. This is another matter which will need consideration at least a year prior to the offering date.

It should be noted that the British Insurance Association Investment Protection Committee (IPC) of the major insurance institutions (as investors) requires that no more than 10 per cent of the ordinary share capital of the company be subject to options or issued under all the employee share schemes (including SAYE schemes) within any period of ten years. To ensure some benefits will be available for future employee participants, the schemes must provide that no more than 3 per cent of the ordinary shares be subject to option or issued under all the employee share schemes in any period of three years. In addition, the National Association of Pension Funds, through its Investment Protection Service, protects members' interests as investors by issuing guidelines concerning acceptable practice in so far as its members are concerned.

If there are existing schemes exceeding the acceptable proportions, the IPCs will usually consider the circumstances of each one and may exceptionally approve them in the case of a company first coming to market.

Pension schemes
The opportunity should be taken to review the pension scheme arrangements in the light of best practice. It may also be wise to have actuarial revaluation of the fund (if a reasonably up-to-date one is not available) to ensure the fund's adequacy or, if there is a material surplus, to decide how that matter shall be dealt with and its consequences for the profit and loss account.

Employee consultation
The Companies Act 1985 requires the company to detail in its annual report what arrangements exist to consult and inform employees about a number of defined criteria. The internal consultancy and communication arrangements should be reviewed not merely for the purposes of satisfying the statutory requirements but for the underlying purpose of employee involvement.

Capital structure
The capitalisation should be reviewed to ensure the simplest possible

capital structure and to consider what should be done with any ordinary shares that do not carry votes.

Taxation

Attempts should be made to bring taxation affairs up to date and reduce potential areas of dispute. The opportunity should be taken to review the company's taxation structure and potential danger areas, such as having inadequate UK taxable profits to allow full recovery of advance corporation tax payments, and foreign taxation implications relative to future business developments.

Insurance

It will be wise to seek an independent review of all insurance arrangements. After several years, it is most likely that circumstances will have changed, with new risks opened up which may have gone undetected. Product liability and trading in foreign countries are points in particular which will need review.

Legal matters

There should be a careful review of issues which are the subject of legal action by and against the company. There should already be procedures in existence for bringing to the attention of senior management any such threatened legal action. If there are not, then procedures should be introduced.

Intellectual property

The opportunity should be taken to review all existing patent and trade mark registrations and to ensure that the company's policies and contractual arrangements are properly in place.

Reporting procedures

It is to be hoped that any company preparing itself for public offering will already have well-established reporting and management information systems. In the unlikely event that this is not so, urgent steps will have to be taken to rectify the omission so that the company can navigate itself properly and deal satisfactorily with the more demanding reporting requirements of public companies. Surprising though it may be, there is evidence even today that management reporting is deficient.

Half-year results

The Stock Exchange requires the announcement of half-yearly results. In this respect it will be wise to review the normal incidence of profits. The announcement of losses at the half-way stage is, on the whole, undesirable. The underlying causes need careful consideration with a view to avoiding the situation if possible, and the preparation of a long-term plan to adjust the balancing of earnings within the accounting year.

The business plan

Reference was made in Chapter 2 to the importance of the business plan. Before a public offering the longer range plan and the underlying strategies and objectives must be subjected to rigorous testing for overall credibility. The plan will justify the growth prospects which must underlie the intent to go public and must have the commitment of all directors and senior managers.

Costs of new issues

Placings can be made at a significantly lower cost than offers for sale, and are far more usual for small issues. And initial issues on the USM are less expensive than on the listed market.

The general aim of the sponsors is to ensure a satisfactory after-market, which usually means that there will be a tendency to offer shares at some discount to the calculated maximum, thus encouraging over-subscription and a price premium in the immediate after-market.

Not surprisingly, there is evidence of economies of scale in new issues. In the listed market, the costs for small issues (say up to £3m) will be approaching 20 per cent, reducing more or less pro rata to about 5 per cent for issues in excess of £10m. For placings, these will be lower because of the absence of sub-underwriting commissions and lower advertising costs. Broadly similar ratio trends apply to USM listings, although there would seem to be greater variation in costs for listing more or less similar amounts.

With rights issues, the expenses for a small amount (say up to £3m) can be expected to be around 8 per cent, reducing to around 4 per cent for amounts in excess of £10m. There may be more competitive charges in the post Big Bang period. And, if the company is willing to lessen the interests of its existing shareholders (because it is now possible to set aside pre-emption rights if shareholder approval is given not more than 12 months before), the company may decide to sell the whole of its proposed issue to a securities house (the bought deal) for it to place the shares with the investors. In this case, it may be possible to secure the issue at low discounts to the market price.

The following costs are likely to be incurred in an offer for sale:

- capital duty

- stock exchange listing fee
- advertising costs
- printing costs
- accountants' fees
- legal fees
- issuing house fees
- sub-underwriting commissions
- brokers' fees.

After quotation

Once a company is brought to the market and shares are publicly quoted, all shareholders are affected by the share price quotations. The Stock Exchange is concerned that there shall be a proper market, that it is conducted in an orderly manner and that all shareholders shall be fairly treated by having access to price-sensitive information at the same time.

For these reasons, the Stock Exchange requires that quoted public companies observe certain formalities which are contained in Stock Exchange undertakings: for listed companies they are described as 'Continuing Obligations for Listed Companies' and for USM companies 'General undertakings for USM companies', both of broadly similar content. A company's failure to comply can lead to suspension of the market quotation. Section 5 of the Stock Exchange 'Yellow Book', which includes these requirements, also contains a model code for securities transactions by directors of a listed company.

With a view to ensuring equal treatment and information the Stock Exchange, and in some cases also the Companies Act 1985 require:

- Immediate disclosure of any information which might influence the price of securities.
- Immediate advice of events which will or may affect prices, eg:

  - significant acquisitions or disposals;
  - changes in the directors;
  - changes in substantial shareholdings;
  - bids for the company and information to be disclosed as required by the City Code for Take-overs and Mergers;
  - purchase by a company of its own redeemable securities;
  - particulars of the holders of 5 per cent or more of any class of shares.

- Prior clearance through the Stock Exchange of all documents to be

issued publicly.
- The preparation of half-yearly accounts which must either be circulated to shareholders or advertised in a national daily newspaper.
- The advice of all dividend declarations.
- The annual report and accounts to be sent to every shareholder.
- Appropriate advice to every shareholder in accordance with the Companies Act 1985 of ordinary and extraordinary meetings.
- The seeking of suspension from quotation if a false market develops arising from information or events which may affect prices, but which cannot be immediately clarified for the fair treatment of all shareholders.

Once a company is quoted, there are inherent dangers of insider trading arising from some parties having access to price-sensitive information which is not simultaneously available to all. All directors and officers of the company must understand these dangers and try to avoid them. In practice this is very difficult because it is inevitable that a number of people always have advance knowledge of events which can sometimes be of a very price-sensitive nature.

The greatest care must also be exercised by directors in dealings with the press and professional analysts. Companies should also have internal policies preventing dealings in their own shares for a defined period in advance of yearly and half-year accounts and when there are dealings by directors, particulars must be lodged with the Stock Exchange.

Directors' responsibilities

There are a number of factors of particular concern to directors of companies which have sought a public quotation. These include:

Warranties
The sponsor will usually require personal warranties from the directors for the matters covered in the listing particulars.

Responsibilities to investors
The possible causes of action which an investor might have against the directors in respect of a prospectus or listing particulars, upon which the investor relied in subscribing for shares, fall into three categories:

- the Financial Services Act 1986

- negligent misstatement
- other causes of action.

Briefly, these are:

Financial Services Act 1986
Under Part IV of this Act, it is the directors' duty to ensure that, after making proper enquiry, they believe that the listing particulars contain all the information that investors (and their professional advisers) would reasonably require and expect to find in order to make an informed judgement of the company's financial position and of the rights attaching to the securities being issued. A number of persons associated with the issue carry that responsibility, including each director who has consented to the issue.

Failure to comply with Part IV of this Act will amount to a breach of statutory duty.

Negligent misstatement
An investor, relying on the information given, might have a claim for damages against the directors for negligent misstatement. To succeed, it would be necessary for the claimant to establish that there was negligence and that he has suffered financial damage by reason of that negligence.

It could also be open to an investor to seek to set aside the contract to acquire shares if induced by material misrepresentation, upon which he has relied, whether fraudulent or innocent, provided he does so within a reasonable time. Although such action would in the first place be against the issuing house or the company, it is most likely that one of those defendants would claim against the directors.

Other causes of action
Claims for damage could arise from a number of other causes. By an investor claiming to be fraudulently induced to apply for shares in a company; claims under the Misrepresentation Act 1967 which, while not necessarily against the directors directly, could arise as a consequence of a claim against the issuing house or the company; claims under the Theft Act 1968 in relation to any written statement containing items of a material nature made with intent to deceive; and under the Financial Services Act 1986 in relation to statements or forecasts made knowingly misleading or false.

120

Distributions

Distributions to shareholders may only be made from realised profits. Profits arising from a revaluation of assets which are unrealised are, therefore, not available for distribution. Nor may distributions be made from current profits unless past losses have first been made good.

Development costs are now the subject of company law. Under Section 269, development costs must be treated as realised losses. For the purpose of determining distributable profits, such costs may only be carried forward if the directors so determine; the financial statements disclose the fact; and the directors explain their reason for such treatment.

Differences between public and private company rules for distributions are referred to in Appendix 5.

Acquisitions and mergers

It is not considered appropriate to try to deal with the complexities of the acquisition and merger of companies in a fundraising context. However, it is relevant in at least the following areas:

- In a reverse take-over, where the principal purpose of the offeror is to acquire a cash-rich company, or one with assets capable of easy realisation into cash.

- In the case of a take-over of one company by another when the main purpose of the acquisition is to acquire cash available in the target company or assets capable of easy realisation into cash.

    The consequence of such an acquisition is similar to a rights issue so far as the acquiring company is concerned. Such an acquisition might be best exemplified by the acquisition of, say, an investment trust, comprising quoted investments and cash or cash instruments. As investment trusts tend to be quoted at a discount in the market, the acquisition may yield a small additional benefit.

- In the case of certain major acquisitions, there may well be the need for substantial funding in order to provide the cash which may be required by the offeror, as part of the bid. Such funding may become available against plans for the target company to be dismembered and sold in packages, yielding in some circumstances a substantial surplus over acquisition price and/or a core investment acquired at a relatively cheap price.

121

Conclusion

Seeking quotation for a company on the Stock Exchange is a significant stage in its development. It is a logical step which nearly always has to be taken when a company reaches a point at which it requires access to more capital than is likely to be forthcoming from private sources. Quotation carries with it much wider responsibilities for the directors, and in many respects involves a significant change in attitudes. The interests of many individual and institutional investors are involved, for which the board assumes primary responsibility. Quotation offers opportunities, but also threats.

There will be few occasions thereafter when the board will feel comfortable without seeking professional legal and accountancy advice, and often also that from bankers and brokers.

It is not a step which can be taken without consideration of all the consequences and implications for the company, its board and management.

Chapter 7
Management Buy-outs

The business environment

A growing feature of the UK financial scene during recent years has been the number of financial arrangements which have been brought about for the purpose of encouraging an existing management to acquire either the company which employs them or a discrete part of that company. These are known as management buy-outs or, in US terminology, 'leveraged buy-outs' because of high gearing which tends to be typical of this type of transaction.

The impetus behind the increased UK activity would seem to stem from the co-incidence of several factors, including:

- The encouragement of a more enterprising business climate, assisted by helpful changes in company and tax laws.
- The more critical analysis of the results of widely spread group companies, or conglomerates. This is the result of a more competitive business climate and the vulnerability to take-over of companies which are underperforming, or whose stock market prices seem to be depressed.

  A more critical attitude to the commercial performance of discrete parts of a group frequently indicates the good sense of hiving off some activities. And with sharpened perception of the benefits from concentration on those core businesses in which the group intends to operate, some activities are likely to be judged as peripheral and available for disposal.

A similar conclusion may result from the take-over of a company which, as part of the acquirer's strategy, is intended to be broken up and sold off in parts.

One of the possible methods of disposal is a buy-out by the government of that activity, with the following benefits:

- The probability of a more motivated performance on the part of a desegregated management which is more self-reliant and has the prospect of capital gain.
- The attractiveness to a financier of a management team with a proven track record.
- The more easily achieved marketing of the bought-out shares through the securities market.

Buy-out variations

There are variations of the general theme, the principal of which are:

- A buy-out may be built around a single director or manager, or it may encompass a management team.
- The mirror of a buy-out is the buy-in. This circumstance comes about as a result of the introduction of new (external) management by the acquiring financier.
- Frequently, as an integral part of the arrangements, not only will the management acquire a substantial shareholding, but company employees will also be given the opportunity to have a share stake in the company on favourable terms. It is increasingly common for management to be rewarded for achieving pre-determined milestones. The initial shareholding, depending on the size of the deal, may be in the range 15 to 25 per cent with the opportunity perhaps to increase the stake by a similar amount on measured performance, known as a ratchet. A variation could be for the initial holding to be reduced on failure to achieve agreed goals.

Motivation of the parties

A company's decision to sell part of its activities and for management to be involved in their acquisition can clearly arise from a number of factors, some of which may be conflicting.

The vendor is likely to reach such a decision because of one or more of the following influences:

- A genuine reappraisal of the group's business strategy, as a result of which the activity to be sold is no longer seen (if ever it was) as of fundamental importance to the achievement of the main objectives and strategies of the group. Concentration on core business activities is now more frequently perceived as being in the interests of the vending group's shareholders.

Relevant factors may include:

- concentration of cash or management resources on fundamentals;
- removing a cash drain because of investment or product development requirements;
- removing a problem activity which is demanding too much cash or management resources, or whose return on investment is damaging group performance. Managed by a dedicated and separated management the prospects may be perceived differently;
- removing a business activity which may no longer have any important synergy for the group;
- removing a company where there is perceived to be substantial risk of failure in the short or medium term;
- realising cash in order to preserve the main business activity.

- Improving the group's profit and earnings-per-share performance with a view to achieving a better stock market rating.
- Improving performance in anticipation of, or under threat from, an unwelcome predator.
- Principal shareholder wishes to realise his investment, particularly in the case of a family company where the principal shareholder is reluctant to sell to a competitor.
- Perceived statutory threat, eg fear of a monopoly commission investigation or in the case of a group with TV broadcasting interests the need to avoid take-over difficulties with, say, the Independent Broadcasting Authority.
- Reverting a public company with a Stock Exchange listing into a private company if a public quotation is no longer relevant or appropriate.

From the point of view of the buyers, it has to be presumed that the overriding interest is personal: either to preserve a threatened job structure or, much more likely, to realise an opportunity to improve their financial position significantly, particularly through capital gain.

There will most probably be higher personal risk for the managers committing to the buy-out; it has to be presumed that they are prepared to accept this risk in exchange for greater control over their own destiny and the calculation that the perceived financial gain will outweigh the risk involved. It therefore follows that a manager putting his resources at risk will not do so unless he believes in the future success of the activity, even if the vendor does not share that optimism.

125

It is quite likely, however, that a competent management working with a reconstructed board will achieve better results than if the activity is relatively unimportant in its existing environment. The instinct for self-preservation is strong. The incentive to a secure financial future is perhaps an unrepeatable opportunity. And, in addition, a more committed work-force, with personal incentive to succeed in a more compact and personal business. A difference in view from that of the vendors is therefore perfectly compatible.

Moreover, the management may believe that they can arrange a more appropriate compensation package if they are not employed as part of a large corporate vehicle. Pension arrangements, for example, may be tailored to individual needs rather than the standardised benefits of a group pension scheme. In this way the sellers and buyers can move towards a mutually satisfactory negotiation.

Key interests

If there is to be a mutually satisfactory deal, the terms and conditions will need to meet the objectives of the three key players:

- the vendor
- the management
- the financier.

As in any successful negotiation, it is always important to try to understand what is essential to each of the parties, and what can be compromised. Success is obviously more likely if the company management and the vending group are on good terms, with mutual respect for each other. It is almost certain that the managers will need professional assistance to bring about the necessary conditions and, indeed, the adviser may take the lead negotiating position.

A number of parties are equipped to assume the overall advisory role. The larger firms of professional accountants, a banker with relevant corporate financial skills or a venture capital specialist seem likely to be the most appropriate. Or perhaps a business broker. The key ingredient, as always, will be the price.

The vendor
If the vendor is a listed company, the special factors it will have in mind will almost certainly include:

- Providing a good public explanation as to why the deal is being made and how it shall be presented.

- Considering the implications of the sale on the parent company accounts, including the loss or gain arising from the proceeds of sale compared with the cost in the books, and the consequences for future trading results.
- Considering the taxation implications and therefore the need to structure the deal in a tax-efficient manner.
- To what extent there will be a continuing relationship with the desegregated business:

  - of a trading nature
  - guarantees to the new company
  - deferred consideration
  - part ownership.

- Transfer of pension benefits for the segregated employees and how a surplus in the pension fund should be handled.
- Risks associated with insider trading knowledge of the disposal.
- There may be a need under Stock Exchange rules for a listed company to issue a circular to its shareholders in respect of a disposal covered as a Class 1 transaction or, more likely, a Class 4 transaction involving a director.

The management
The management's interests will embrace:

- buying the activity at the cheapest available price and ensuring that the future return on investment will meet the new management objectives.
- seeking assurance concerning continuing customer relations when a separated company;
- the extent of their control over the new company;
- the extent to which the management will have to be 'on risk' by personal financial commitment required by the financier;
- the structure of the board and management ability to work easily with new directors;
- ensuring that the separated business will be viable, able to withstand the pressure without parental support, and with adequate cash generation to meet future financial and development obligations;
- seeking from the vendor appropriate guarantees and indemnities;
- deciding how to replace any services or support previously provided on a group basis, eg accounting, computers, purchasing;
- ensuring the rights necessary to ongoing trading are transferred eg

trade mark and patent rights either by way of acquisition or licence;

- their confidence in being able to meet performance targets agreed with the financier and probably necessary to secure enhanced long-term share ownership geared to performance;
- plans for realisation in due course, either through quotation or other method;
- personal taxation.

The financier

The financier will seek to be satisfied that:

- The management is competent and likely to have the qualities needed to operate as a separate business.
- The business plans are credible, realistic and able to support the future cash and profit requirements.
- There is a satisfactory 'exit' plan.
- The return to the financier will meet his internal objectives. It is most likely that he will view the return as a combination of an income stream and a capital stream (and there may be preferences as to which has the greater weighting) viewed together over a period of years. The financier will almost certainly expect an overall cumulative return during the investment period of not less than 30 per cent per annum.
- The investment will in all other respects satisfy his internal portfolio guidelines for risk, spread of investment and the like.
- The likely future requirements for capital.
- The board is well structured and balanced. The financier will almost certainly reserve the right to board representation by one or two people.
- There are adequate safety nets to permit influence if the proposition starts to go wrong. A shareholder agreement will most likely be a feature of the deal.

The business plan

As we have seen, the preparation of a sound business plan is the kernel of the proposition. And, because the management comes with the business, the plan should be developed on a thoroughly realistic basis, including sound knowledge of its strengths and weaknesses, the opportunities open to it and the competitive threats existing and likely to develop. The structure of such a plan is fully set out in Appendix 3.

The most important (and difficult) assessment usually relates to the market situation: its size and structure; the company products and their relative strengths and weaknesses in the intended market; the plans and capability to develop new products and to innovate; the probability of technical enhancements. It can and should be expected that the financier will want to understand these issues fully and to be satisfied that they really do hang together. To satisfy himself, he may well employ his own independent market and technical advisers.

The market is the key element in the plan, but certainly not the only element. Appendix 3 identifies the many technical, logistical and financial aspects which must be considered and interrelated to produce a well-written and credible proposal.

From this plan will emerge the planned:

- profit and revenue accounts
- balance sheets
- cash flows
- financial requirements
- key financial ratios.

As an absolute minimum, the plan must be for two years, preferably at least three, and up to five. As the horizon extends, detail will assume less importance, but within the main business strategy year by year the following should emerge:

- objectives
- projected revenues
- projected margins
- projected capital employed
- key financial ratios

The plan will demonstrate:

- the competence of the management to foresee the future business, and plan comprehensively to achieve it;
- the commercial viability of the business;
- the ability to structure a sound financial proposition.

Finally, the effects of taxation must be properly thought through and evaluated.

Legal considerations and structure

Brief consideration must be given to some of the legal issues associated

129

with the provision of financial assistance to managers for the purpose of acquiring shares in the company that employs them.

Although management can be involved in the acquisition of a subsidiary company from its parent company, it may be equally true of a private company whose owner wishes to release part or all of his share interest by selling to the existing management.

This may be more practical, as well as more considerate, than selling to an unknown buyer or seeking a quotation (which may not be appropriate). In the case of a group, the subsidiary may be already operating as an entity. If it is not, it will be necessary for the parent to form a new company to acquire the discrete business which is to be sold.

It is a feature of nearly all management buy-outs that the management is not in a position wholly to finance the purchase of the shares to be acquired. Prior to 1985, there were difficulties in arranging finance for this purpose because it was illegal for a company (except under Section 54 of the Companies Act 1948 for the making of loans to employees other than directors) to provide any financial assistance for the purchase of its own shares. Thus, for example, it was illegal for a bank to lend to directors the funds required to purchase their employer's shares if part of the transaction involved (as it usually would) the company's assets being caught by the bank's security provisions for the loan. The 1985 Act has modified that position.

There is, under Section 151 of the Companies Act 1985, a general prohibition against a company giving financial assistance (widely defined) for the purpose of purchasing its own shares or those of its holding company, whether before, at the same time as, or after the shares are acquired.

Thus there is no prohibition against:

- a subsidiary company providing financial assistance for the purchase of shares in a fellow subsidiary company;
- a holding company providing financial assistance for the purchase of shares in one of its subsidiaries.

The provision of financial assistance is lawful in the following circumstances:

- If the financial assistance is given in good faith in the interests of the company and the principal purpose of the arrangement is not to give financial assistance; or, if the giving of that financial assistance is only an incidental purpose of the arrangement.
- Distribution of assets by a company by way of dividend (or in a winding up) where the proceeds are used to buy shares in the

130

company.

- Where the funds arise from a reduction of the company capital (by approval of the court) or a purchase or redemption of shares lawfully made under Chapter VII of Part V of the 1985 Act.
- The making of loans to employees (other than directors) with a view to those persons beneficially acquiring fully paid-up shares in the company or its holding company. The rules for a private company are less stringent than for a public company and, in particular, a private company is not caught by the 'principal purpose rule' outlined above. This means that a private company could provide financial assistance as the principal purpose of an arrangement, although there are some rules concerning the financial condition of the company providing the assistance which effectively requires it to be solvent before and after the transaction. The management may be required to warrant 12 months' solvency.

There is a further constraint on a private company providing financial assistance for the purchase of shares in its holding company if that company is a public company: in that event, the 'principal purpose rule' will continue to apply.

The procedures are, however, complex. Clearly, good legal and accountancy advice are essential.

The interests of the participating parties were outlined earlier. There are some further commercial aspects likely to need consideration, as follows:

- It is most unlikely that the management will be able to find most of the money required. But they will be expected by the principal financier to be at some personal risk to ensure commitment and responsibility. Financiers' views differ as to the extent of management exposure, but it is probably wise not to push personal involvement so hard as to cause the individuals constant concern about their risks.
- The financier may not wish to have such an interest in the voting shares of the company that the target company will be a subsidiary company. Attitudes vary, but current trends are perhaps tending towards initial majority control, with a reduction of shareholding through the operation of ratchets, thus rewarding management a larger stake on performance achievement. He will give careful consideration as to whether he wishes to hold in excess of 20 per cent, the consequence of which normally involves equity accounting by the holder. Perhaps between 20 and 40 per cent might be

appropriate. He will probably give some consideration to the desirability of using an 'offshore' vehicle for his investment. Arrangements have now been made with the Inland Revenue to permit limited partnerships 'onshore'.

- The management will want to reap the rewards if they make a success of the business. The financier has a similar interest because he wants the management to create a successful business and thus get adequate recompense for the risks involved.

  It will therefore be usual to offer some capital opportunity to management. This may take the form of option rights (either against the company and/or the financier) geared to performance criteria agreed between the parties or to an increase in the proportion of the management share interest on the achievement of predetermined goals. It is most likely that the trigger points will be determined by equity market capitalisation or on an earnings-per-share calculation. Such events may be associated with exit from the investment, or related to events determined in the business plan or on cash flows.

  Careful consideration will need to be given to the taxation implications whichever methods are adopted.

- It is worth exploring the extent to which the vendor is willing to retain a share interest in the company. As part of the financial arrangements it may be possible to negotiate that part of the consideration payable to the vendor is deferred over a period of time. Attractive participation rights may form part of the deferred payment.

- For the reasons given, because the management financial contribution will be relatively slight, but the ownership proportion substantial, the business will be more highly geared than might normally be regarded as prudent. Loan capital or perhaps redeemable preference shares are likely to to held by the financier to bridge the gap.

  The loan capital could carry the right to partial or total conversion into equity. This will provide a fallback in the event of performance being less than planned and allow the financier to assume substantial equity rights under those circumstances if he so wishes.

  The implication is that there will need to be substantial positive cash flows to permit the servicing of loans or preference shares and their repayment in accordance with the terms of the arrangement. It may be visualised that ordinary shares shall be redeemed from company cash flows: this can be one method of increasing the ratio of the management's share interest. Alternatively, it is likely that votes will attach to preference shares held by the financier in the event that there is a material breach of the issue conditions, thus reducing management's ratio.

- Ensuring that there has been full disclosure of all material facts before the sale.

The above, together with taxation considerations (which may be complicated), will substantially govern the financial structure of the arrangement, and may well point to the most practical solution as being the formation of a new (holding) company for the purpose of acquiring the company to be bought-out, or its assets.

It is likely that there will be a shareholder agreement to ensure that the financier, carrying the major risk, can protect his interests and influence the conduct of the company, in addition to appointing one or two directors to the board, as is usual.

Depending on the extent of the risk, it is quite likely that the principal financier will work in concert with other financiers on a syndicated basis, and/or with non-financial interests.

The presentation

The importance of the business plan has been stated. From it, the management will be in a position to put together an effective presentation for the finance house, and be able to deal confidently with the detailed discussions which are bound to ensue if the first hurdle is overcome. But that first hurdle does have to be crossed, and it is therefore important to spend time on a good presentation and to obtain good professional financial advice at an early stage. The matters of greatest interest to the finance house will include:

- The corporate objectives.
- The directors and senior management.
- The market analysis.
- The strategy for securing the marketing objectives; and in particular product planning, product benefits, the strengths and weaknesses of the company, the opportunities and competitive threats.
- The technical capability to create new products and to innovate.
- The organisational structure.
- The facilities or logistical plan.
- The plan for communications.

- Profit and revenue plans for the next two years and an outline of the following three years and capital expenditure plans. Balance sheets at key points.
- Cash flows pre and post tax, showing their adequacy for servicing loan and preference capital.
- Financial requirements and timing, and proposals for capital and borrowing requirements.
- Taxation implications, including unusual taxation features.
- Key financial ratios.
- Planned exit route and an indication of the overall financial reward to the financier.

How the presentation is to be made, the use of visual aids and the involvement of cross sections of the managers in the presentation must be carefully considered. First impressions are very important. Therefore, the timing (keep it brief), the location (make it convenient) and a rehearsal are all important. The management is selling itself, as well as a financial proposal.

Consideration should also be given to the type of questions likely to be raised and to obtaining independent endorsement of important elements (eg, patent protection or technical issues).

Business managers often do not give sufficient thought to the importance of establishing in the mind of the financier at the first business discussion a feeling that the project is inherently interesting and deserves support, and that the management really knows what it is doing.

Illustration

A balance sheet after buy-out might look like this:

	£
Assets	
Fixed	400,000
Working capital	600,000
	1,000,000
Share Capital	
Ordinary shares of 100p	
Management 55%	55,000
Financier 45%	45,000
	100,000
10% Redeemable preference shares	100,000

Loan Capital

Bank loan of 12½% secured	400,000
15% Subordinated loan with conversion rights (financier)	400,000
	1,000,000

Suppose turnover is £3m pa in year 1 (ie assets turning three times) with pre-tax, pre-interest profit of 12.5 per cent (ie £375,000).

Interest costs will be:

	£
Secured loan	48,000
Subordinated loan	60,000
	108,000

This implies overall interest cover of about three times, and for the secured loan about eight times, and should be acceptable to any financier. It is possible that lower cover could be acceptable in the first and second years. The extent of asset cover will also be considered in assessing the risk. The 'leveraged' buy-out clearly involves taking risks with high gearing.

The preference dividend is also a prior charge on distributed profits – in this example £10,000 pa.

Capital repayment requirements may be:

	£
Redeemable preference shares (perhaps to commence in year 3)	20,000
Bank loan (7 years)	57,000
	77,000

Now let us suppose that the plan over five years indicates annual turnover growth of 20 per cent and net pre-tax margin rising to 15 per cent pre-interest, then at the end of year 5 the profit and loss account will show:

	£
Turnover	6,200,000
Pre-tax profit	930,000
less interest	81,000
(bank loan end year 4, £228,000)	
	849,000
Assumed tax charge at 35%	297,000
Net profit after tax	552,000
Valuation: (say) 12 times earnings	6,620,000
less: preference shares (say, 3 years redeemed)	70,000
EQUITY VALUE	6,550,000

Management share	3,602,500
Financier's share	2,947,500
The financier's investment is:	
Ordinary shares	45,000
Subordinated loan	400,000
	445,000

Over 5 years his loan interest will have been	300,000
And the capital value is	2,947,500
Combined	3,247,500
A 30% annual return would, over 5 years, imply an exit value of	1,650,000
The indicated value will give an overall yield approaching	50% per annum

Management incentive

To illustrate the effects of a ratchet, suppose the agreement between management and financier had provided management incentive along the following lines:

Management to benefit by increased shareholding if the capital value at year 5 were:

between £6m and £7m	5%
over £7m	10%

In the illustration, the capital value has achieved the minimum, but falls within the lower bracket of capital values. Management share will therefore be increased by 5 per cent raising it to 60 per cent.

Financier – loan conversion

Let it be further assumed that the financier may, at his option, convert the subordinated loan into ordinary shares as follows:

EPS	Loan £ conversion factor
less than 300p	5 for 1 share
Between 300 and 400p	10 for 1
Between 400 and 500p	20 for 1
over 500p	40 for 1

Profits after tax, and after providing for a preference divedend of, say £7,000, would be £545,000, which gives an EPS of:

$$\frac{£545,000}{100,000} = 545p$$

As achieved EPS is over 500p, the financier may convert the £400,000 subordinated loan into:

$$\frac{400,000}{40} = 10,000 \text{ shares}$$

Assuming 100 per cent conversion the revised shareholding will then be:

	Shares	
	Financier	Management
As adjusted for management incentive	40,000	60,000
Shares issued against loan conversion	10,000	
	50,000	60,000
Revised ratios	45.5%	54.5%

It should be noted that, with the loan converted, the profits after tax will increase as follows:

	£
As stated, after tax	552,000
Adjustment for loan interest:	
£60,000 less tax at 35%	39,000
	591,000
Less: Preference dividend say	7,000
Attributable to ordinary shares	584,000
Shares in issue	110,000
Revised EPS	531p

It will be noted that the value of the business has been calculated on its earnings. This is the most significant factor affecting values. If the share is quoted on the market, the capitalisation will be determined by the market. But if not, it is likely to be based on similar considerations adjusted for perceived future earnings prospects.

The essential elements in the capitalisation calculation therefore are:

- the pre- and post-tax earnings
- the multiple to be applied to post-tax earnings.

Asset values should not figure prominently in the valuation unless some special factors are involved, for example, land which may be far more valuable for an alternative use. It is quite likely that the going concern value of the business will exceed book values, thus representing a 'goodwill' element. In the case of a service business, it is likely that the goodwill will represent a substantial sum because the asset base may well be quite modest. For that reason, a lower price earnings ratio may be appropriate becaue the business is entirely dependent upon the intellectual skills of the management and therefore more vulnerable to mobility or other personal factors. There is no doubt that financiers feel more comfortable if there is a substantial asset base. Whatever the book value, however, the real value as a going concern is dependent on the viability and earnings of the business. It always comes back to the management issue.

Taxation

It will not be surprising if the parties to a management buy-out have differing taxation interests. For the management, the imperative must be to seek the most competent professional advice that can be obtained. It is particularly in the initial stages that advice is required, so that the structure of the deal can be influenced to take account of the taxation factors although, in the final analysis, the commercial interests must always be the deciding factor if there is a straight conflict. Because the taxation interests of the other parties may not coincide with those of the management, it is probable that some of the desirable elements may not be achievable. Those which are essential must be identified.

A brief review of some of the relevant considerations is set out below, although the manner in which the deal is structured will obviously have different taxation implications.

The vendor
- If the vendor is a group for taxation purposes, the consequences of a disposal of a subsidiary will need review. It is possible that the disposal of a profitable business might mean that losses elsewhere in the group cannot thereafter be fully relieved. Normally, profits or losses are apportioned on a time basis to the date of sale but, if this were to result in a distortion, 'a just and reasonable method' more fairly reflecting a fair solution may be used.
- It is also possible that the disposal of a profitable subsidiary liable to corporation tax could adversely affect the full recovery of ACT paid on the group's distributions.

- If the sale is of the business, the apportionment of the sale price across the different types of asset must be considered.
- If the business and its assets are sold, rather than the shareholding in the company, there may be balancing charges on those assets which have been subject to capital allowances.
- Capital gains tax will arise on the sale of the shares if a profit is made on the investment; or on assets sold, and goodwill, in excess of original cost if the transaction is a disposal of the business rather than the company.
- Consideration will need to be given to stripping out excess cash prior to the sale, in the form of a distribution. This will have the effect of reducing the value of the company for sale.

The purchaser (management and financier)

- If the sale is of the company, tax losses brought forward may be available for relief against future profits, but there are restrictive criteria concerning any change in the trade to which the losses are attributable; such change may be brought about, for example, by closure of a factory and merging into an existing factory, or changes in product range. Losses brought forward will not be available if the sale is of the business alone.
- There are a number of anti-avoidance provisions which may be applicable, arising from the relationships between the management and the vendor.
- The greatest care is necessary in the purchase of shares or the granting of options in the company which will become the employer.

    The Inland Revenue will seek to tax any capital benefits arising as an income tax liability (as opposed to capital gains) on the grounds that the benefits are employment related.
- Consideration will also have to be given to the 'close' company provisions. A 'close' company is, broadly, one under the control of five or fewer persons and their close family connections. A quoted company will not be close if 35 per cent or more of the shares are publicly quoted. If a company is close, interest on borrowings by the shareholders for the purchase of shares should be available for tax relief. And the Inland Revenue can attribute investment income to the shareholders, whether distributed or not, but not the trading income. This is to limit tax avoidance.
- The shareholders' tax objectives should be to arrange matters so that relief is available against business failure by obtaining:

- capital gains tax relief on loans not repaid by the company
- income tax relief on losses on shareholdings.

- It may be possible to make shareholding in an eligible company attractive through the availability of income tax relief arising from the Business Expansion Scheme. As outlined in Appendix 4 such relief is not available to employees, paid directors or shareholders owning more than 30 per cent. The financier may not wish to accept such constraints, or he may consider that the future development of the business would be adversely affected (or that there will be a breach of the conditions giving rise to tax clawback).

- If there is more than one company comprising a group, the necessary conditions concerning ownership (75 per ce.ˑt control) must be complied with if group tax reliefs are to be available.

- Consideration should be given by individuals to the future implications of inheritance tax; for example, the manner in which shares in the company are beneficially owned. Any rearrangement of personal affairs is best done when the initial investment is made.

- Warranties by the vendor will be required, which will include undisclosed income and capital gains tax liabilities.

- There is always the possibility that some of the shares will be held in some form of trust which may be 'offshore', ie outside the UK tax net, as indeed a direct shareholding by a foreign owner may be. Cases are known where the financier requires small shareholdings to be held initially in a voting trust set up for that purpose in order to simplify shareholder decision-taking.

Future trading

After a management buy-out, the company's competence to trade, and its markets, will almost certainly be as they were prior to the arrangement. But it is not necessarily just the same from the point of view of third parties. The removal of the security, or perceived security, and trading benefits arising from a group relationship, can be very important to creditors and others trading with the company.

Because it will be standing alone, favourable group trading terms may not continue to be available. Creditors may perceive the company as a less satisfactory credit risk. This possibility should be foreseen and allowed for in the business plan.

Similarly, some customers may not be willing to trade with the newly separated company because of uncertainty whether it will succeed or continue to offer future product security through appropriate levels of research and development expenditure. Clearly, attempts will be made to secure assurances on this vital point before closing the deal, but care will be necessary to avoid premature disclosure for many reasons, not least the need to ensure proper communication with employees to a planned timetable and the avoidance of a false market in the shares in the case of a quoted company. Some of these risks may be minimised by securing vendor company guarantees for a period of time after the transaction, or by the vendor continuing an association with the company through a (minority) shareholding.

Mention has already been made of the need for the separated company to consider the future non-availability of services previously provided on a group basis. These are most likely to arise from group advice or services relating to finance including taxation, legal, procurement, research and development, personnel, pension, computers and public relations. Much depends on the extent to which the bought-out company was self-managing.

The group may or may not have been properly recovering the cost of such services from its subsidiaries or the cost may not have been allocated fairly across subsidiaries. In any event, the future cost of such services may be substantially higher (but not necessarily so) if they have to be purchased from independent sources or set up internally.

Arrangements with the vendor should include co-operation on all press, public relations and advertising in so far as it relates to the buy-out. While this will be particularly relevant before and at the time of completion, it will be ongoing for some time.

Perhaps the most important consideration is that of the managers and employees. It is vital that the essential employee team is retained intact. The separation may cause doubts about future trading prospects and security of employment. Everything possible should be done to counter such natural fears. Communication and involvement, always of the greatest importance, will have a high priority, including careful presentation of the business plan, arrangements for transferring pension scheme benefits, plans for employee share option schemes, as well as the inclusion on favourable terms in the buy-out company shareholdings.

Conclusion

The good sense and evident commercial advantages of buy-outs by experienced management are reflected in the growing number of such transactions. Subsequent financial failure has been insignificant, although a longer period of experience through economic cycles is probably required to make a sound judgement.

This chapter will, however, have given some indications of the complex nature of buy-out arrangements, and the need for high quality professional advice in a number of key areas.

As in all fundraising, it is important that the management recognise, and are prepared for, the long and tedious negotiations with a large number of commercial and professional parties which are an unavoidable element in such deals. And to remember that the satisfactory completion of the negotiation is only the beginning of the real task ahead.

Chapter 8
Franchising

While not yet achieving in the UK the popularity that it has in the USA, franchising does represent a different method of business financing and, in appropriate cases, should be considered. The same basic business analysis must first be done, with the end result a properly thought through business plan and a funding proposal.

The meaning of franchise

A franchise arises when one party (the franchisor) grants to another (the franchisee) a licence to make use of all the elements required to set up a business and operate it in accordance with the requirements of the franchisor. The franchisee will be responsible for raising his own funds to run the business, and in consideration for the services provided to make payments to the franchisor, which usually consist of an up-front payment and periodic payments throughout the licence period.

The common characteristics of a franchise are:

- The operation of a particular type of business.
- The use of a specified name, the property of the franchisor.
- The requirement that the franchisee operates the business to a strict format and style prescribed by the franchisor throughout the licence period
- The obligation on the franchisor to provide facilities and services to the franchisee, generally including advice concerning organisation, management, training and merchandising.
- To offer the franchisee the benefit of favourable terms for the purchase of equipment, purchases of materials and supplies and other specified services.

It will be evident, therefore, that a licensed business is likely to be one which lends itself to replication, standardisation and, perhaps most important, recognition. It will not usually be evident to the customer whether a business conforming with such criteria is a branch organisation trading on similar principles or whether it is a franchise. The principal difference is that, in the case of a franchise, the franchisee is effectively in self-employment running his own business and responsible for funding it, compared with a branch manager who is an employee and does not carry financing risks.

For this reason, the franchisee will need to be satisfied that there are certain safeguards built into the franchise agreement to protect his investment. And because such restrictive practices may fall foul of UK and EEC laws, care will need to be exercised and good legal advice obtained.

Commercial benefits

The perceived commercial benefits focus on the opportunity to exploit a marketable proposition through the energies and motivation which can be expected to flow from self-employed businesses, each maximising profits from their own location and applying in the process more ingenuity and customer appeal than might be expected from a full-time employee manager.

Moreover, because the franchisee is responsible for his own funding, the franchisor is likely to be able to expand the business more rapidly on a national scale with the minimum capital investment.

The franchise package

The franchisor must first work out the total formula in detail and prove it under operational conditions in at least one site, preferably more. Simplicity and standardisation are likely to be key elements for successful business. With practical working knowledge the franchisor can package the concept:

- the siting criteria: absolutely key as in all retail operations;
- the ideal design, layout and operational area;
- merchandising assistance, lighting and signing to provide a recognisable image;
- operational assistance through the provision of operating manuals;
- staffing, standards and training requirements;
- administrative and financial systems and reports.

It will almost certainly be a requirement that the franchisee buys his supplies from the franchisor, thus ensuring not only an income stream but also quality control and bulk purchasing advantages.

It will also be likely that the necessary fixtures, fittings and equipment will be available from nominated suppliers on negotiated terms to the franchisor's specification.

Finally, when a number of locations have been secured, the franchisor will be able to offer advertising and promotional advantages on a regional or national scale, depending on the spread of franchised operations.

The franchisee will typically be unskilled in the particular business. The advantage to him, therefore, is a business concept and formula bought as a package, offering him the opportunity to get into business with significantly less risk. Part of the franchisor's concern will be to have competent operators, since much of the financial consideration is payable on the basis of turnover. Clearly it is not in the franchisor's interest to have unsuccessful operators working under his flag. He will therefore be very careful about the selection and training of the franchisee, upon whom he will be so dependent for his future earnings.

The principal disadvantages lie with the risk that one or other of the parties will not carry out his part of the bargain in full. Both parties are mutually dependent upon good performance if the commercial advantages are to be reaped. For these reasons the franchisor may well decide to develop his business in phases:

1. Pilot operation(s) to prove the concepts; to provide 'show' facilities; to work out the operating procedures and write the manuals.
2. Regional developments within a limited range of the franchisor's base, to ensure personal supervision and maintain close control in the early development stages.
3. National development.
4. Possibly, if appropriate, international development.

Financing

Both parties will need financial support. The preparation and presentation of the proposal will accord with usual practice. The franchisor's requirements will be primarily concerned with establishing the proving models, the development of the business, the costs of setting up the ingredients of the package to be offered, and provision for ongoing product development in anticipation of changing needs.

So far as the franchisee is concerned, his requirements will be conditioned by the up-front franchise payment, the start-up costs of equipping premises, recruiting and training staff, and the operating losses which are likely to occur in the early months of trading. If the franchise is concerned with retailing, the correct selection of the site will be the most important decision to be made. If, however, it is a service business, the site location is relatively unimportant. But the use of appropriate vehicles, communication and selection of service staff are critical.

Taxation

The essence of the taxation treatment depends upon the nature of the expense incurred. If it is of a capital nature it will not be allowed, but there will be a writing down allowance in respect of qualifying capital expenditure. Expenditure which is incurred prior to the commencement of trading may not be relieved for tax purposes, but in certain circumstances relief may be granted under Section 39 of the Finance Act 1980.

As franchise arrangements differ, the up-front payment will need to be segregated into its component parts. To the extent that it includes a fee 'for the grant of the licence', however, there will be no allowance.

It will also be necessary to seek information about the nature of annual licence fees which, in some cases, may include payments from which tax should be deducted by the franchisee.

Because the technicalities are important, the franchisee must seek good tax advice.

Conclusion

Franchising in the UK is a significant and growing practice. Properly arranged, it can offer the advantages of marketing and trademarking on a national scale with the entrepreneurial energies of a local self-employed operator more sensitive to the needs of his local customers. It may also offer opportunities for rapid exploitation of the market without the considerable central management and capital resources required by a traditionally structured business. It can therefore be expected that franchising will assume a much more recognised role in the UK, for both goods and services.

Chapter 9
The Causes of Business Failure

Management

The overwhelming cause of business failure lies with management. Failure to understand, or to understand sufficiently early, what is happening in the business and the market-place, and failure to react correctly and rapidly enough to the business environment, which is dynamic and sometimes fast moving.

Good management will avoid most of the these dangers. It will do so within the following general framework:

- Well-selected managers who are skilled, qualified and committed to the business and able to work together as a team.
- A sound planning process, establishing clearly the objectives of the business together with the strategy and plans to achieve them.
- A sound and timely reporting system, so that management is always informed about the important elements in the current situation and how the business is progressing against the plan.
- An ability to take early decisions and action to correct deviations.
- Recognition of the vital necessity of cash flow and cash control

Insufficiency of cash

The most invariable trigger point for business failure is insufficient cash. This means that liabilities falling due in the ordinary course of business cannot, at some point in time, be paid. The impact is likely to be felt most immediately by an inability to pay the weekly wages.

Creditors will normally exercise some tolerance in the event of their invoices not being paid on time. Indeed, that may form part of the trading policy of certain debtors, to seek to defer for quite extended periods the payments which are overdue. Depending upon the financial strength or critical trading relationship that exists, late payment may have to be accepted as the price for a worthwhile trading situation. However, if any of the creditors perceive that overdue payment arises from financial stringency, it is likely that the pressures will increase and escalate, possibly leading to court action for recovery.

Vigilant management who are being properly informed about the state of their business should be aware of the difficulties long before the crunch actually arises. Armed with this foreknowledge, there are steps open to deal positively with the situation. Resorting to further borrowing, if available, can only be acceptable provided there are reasonable prospects that the underlying causes of the growing cash crisis can be satisfactorily resolved.

For this reason, rapidly available information concerning working capital, profitability, orders and margins will in every case be essential. So will the preparation of regular cash forecasts and their comparison with the plan.

There are a number of circumstances in which cash difficulties are likely to arise. They include:

Inadequate control over the working capital
As we have seen, working capital comprises essentially:

- stocks
- debtors
- less trade creditors, and other creditors falling due in the short term.

There are essentially two different circumstances. The first relates to stocks and debtors which are forming a higher and growing ratio in relation to turnover. These are significant danger signs. Therefore, there must be regular information to management concerning stock levels and their composition, including information relating to obsolescence and slow moving lines.

The second is the growth in absolute terms of stocks and debtors, because of expanding business, but not in ratio terms. This is a totally different type of problem, although if not dealt with may have the same end result. A careful watch on average debtor days outstanding, and likewise periods of trade credit, should be undertaken. Whether those periods are broadly similar will depend on a number of factors generally related to the relative strength of the trading parties.

There is one other danger point. If any one customer forms too large a proportion of the debtors, there is significant risk of a damaging cash shortage in the event of debtor failure. For guidance, any single account in excess of 10 per cent should be constantly monitored for creditworthiness. In any case, strong credit control policies should be monitored regularly for correct implementation. There is not quite the same risk from large creditor positions, but trading dangers do exist in the event of supplier failure, particularly if they are specialist or there is no easily available alternative. Taking extended credit from suppliers without their agreement also carries dangers: cut off by suppliers can be very damaging and disruptive. Insurance protection against debtor failure may be available in some cases.

Businesses having high fixed operating costs

This may particularly apply to service companies, such as bus operations and hotels. High 'break-even' points mean that profits emerge only at a substantial revenue level, although in some cases working capital may be quite modest.

Dangers associated with over-trading are not as well understood as they should be. Reference was made on page 148 to the reflection of increased trading by the growth in working capital requirements, even if under proper control and within policy ratio standards which should be determined by the board.

The reason is this. Working capital forms a reasonably constant ratio to turnover, but varies quite widely between one business and another. In some cash-driven businesses there may be no need for working capital, since cash receipts precede creditor payments. In manufacturing businesses, however, the working capital may fall within the range of 25 to 30 per cent of turnover. With rising turnover associated with a rapidly expanding business, there will be the need for very careful cash forecasting and control on individual components of the working capital mix. Short-term bank financing may be appropriate, but the banker may not be entirely compliant. He will expect to see part of the increased working capital provided from company resources.

One of the dangers arising from a rapidly increasing turnover may be in the trading policy being pursued to achieve the turnover increase. For example, the search for larger market share may involve cutting margins. This may be a perfectly acceptable policy provided the net contribution is absolutely higher and the fixed overheads are being controlled within an acceptable ratio to turnover. 'Buying' turnover, however, carries inherent dangers and requires constant vigilance.

Provided net trading margin is at an acceptable and planned level, it should be possible with proper foresight to arrange adequate finance. This may include factoring the debtors as a perfectly sensible method of reducing cash pressure.

The level of fixed overhead also deserves proper vigilance. A rising ratio spells danger. Any sudden deterioration in turnover can have immediate impact on the cash situation because fixed overheads, by their nature, cannot rapidly respond to downward pressure. The monthly expense 'run rate' (the term applied to the rate at which normal operating expenses are incurred) should, therefore, be promptly reported, together with short-term forecasts of the break-even turnover necessary to cover it.

Unbalanced development projects

It should be a cardinal rule that projects, however potentially attractive, should not be entertained if their failure – for any reason – will imperil the total business. This can happen in large companies, as well as small. Just going that bit too far, through inadequate analysis of the project, failure to appreciate the danger points, or changes in uncontrollable external factors can bring about a situation which rapidly results in uncontrollable haemorrhage.

It is therefore very important that the most thorough analysis of the project and the risk should be completed before commitment. Should a judgement be to proceed, it is wise to phase the project, committing cash to the next phase only when there has been satisfactory completion of the earlier one. This means, therefore, the ability to break down the project into recognisable stages, and strong project management. Some computer projects fall into the same category of risk. In the case of property developments, it is usual to finance the development with short-term borrowings, provided they are replaced by appropriate long-term funding on completion (except, perhaps, where the property company is essentially a dealer, rather than an investor).

The dangers are two. A long pre-development period while site factors are being sorted out may take years, and short-term financing will be inappropriate. And change in circumstances, such as unforeseen delays in construction, rising interest rates or a less satisfactory market resulting in lower rentals than expected. All these can produce a rapidly deteriorating financial situation for company and financier, as evidenced by the property and banking crash in the early 1970s.

Over-borrowing

Excessive borrowing carries high risk. 'Excessive' is a relative term, not in absolute amounts. Excessive borrowing arises when the ratio of borrowings to shareholders' funds is too high. What is too high a ratio will depend partly on the nature of the business. A company with a substantial asset base is different from a service company with few physical assets. A company with zero borrowings is almost certainly not maximising its shareholders' returns. A company with 100 per cent borrowings, ie a ratio of 1:1 is, in general, too highly geared. The practical working ratio, therefore, is probably within the range of one-third to two-thirds of shareholders' funds. Against the attractiveness of high shareholder returns arising from substantial borrowings, there are two primary risks:

- The income cover for interest payable may be too low. If that is the situation, any deterioration in the trading position (at contribution level) will have rapid impact on the interest cover which is, of course, an element in the fixed costs.
- Some previously unforeseen element causes a failure to meet a borrowing repayment obligation on time. Such a serious event may have immediate impact on the whole business, particularly if the borrowing is secured.

If, therefore, borrowings are approaching danger level, plans will be required either to realise assets to achieve liquidity or to increase shareholders' funds to restore a more prudent borrowing ratio.

As seen in Chapter 3, the banker's view about asset cover is almost certainly different from what appears on the balance sheet. Effectively, the banker looks at the situation from the point of view of realisation, so that intangible assets (particularly those without a transferable value) will be ignored; stocks will be examined for realisable value (consider, for example, obsolescent stocks or spare parts for a servicing business); debtors for adequate provisions against non-collection. Even in the case of a property, the bank will not normally, in prudence, be willing to lend more than around 65 to 75 per cent of its market valuation. It can therefore be assumed that the banker will want regular, routine information about the working capital movements, and the company should prepare regular, internal statements of the borrowing ratios and the asset cover calculated on banking principles.

Under-capitalisation

This is substantially the mirror image of over-borrowing, but there are certain differences.

As seen in Chapter 3, short-term borrowings should not be used for acquiring fixed or long-term assets. This means, therefore, that the shareholders' funds must be adequate at least to provide:

- for fixed capital requirements;

- for a proportion of the working capital requirements;
- for planned developments;
- a proper ratio to borrowings. Long-term borrowings will be appropriate in many cases, in lieu of shareholders' funds, but they will form part of the overall borrowing ratio.

The principal sources of increased capital are:

- internally generated after tax profits (subject, of course, to any extraordinary losses not charged against normal revenue) and to dividend payments;
- new capital introduced.

Legal consequences

In closing this chapter, mention must be made of directors' responsibility either under various provisions of the Companies Act 1985 or the Insolvency Act 1986 insofar as financial failure is concerned. Responsibilities have been significantly widened by the latter legislation.

Directors can now have a personal liability to contribute to the assets of a company which has gone into insolvent liquidation by order of the court on application by the liquidator. A company can, of course, go into solvent liquidation without such personal risk arising, ie the company has sufficient assets to pay its debts and the expenses of winding up.

The key to potential liability for wrongful trading arises 'if, at some time before the commencement of liquidation, the director knew, or ought to have concluded, that there was no reasonable prospect of avoiding an insolvent liquidation'. And there will be good defence provided the directors can satisfy the court that 'he took every step with a view to minimising the potential loss to the company's creditors as he ought to have taken'. The Insolvency Act defines the circumstances which are relevant in considering whether the steps taken were, under the circumstances, satisfactory and such as would have been taken by 'a reasonably intelligent person'.

The penalties for fraudulent trading, which can extend beyond the directors, will of course be more severe, and in either case can involve disqualification from being concerned in the management of a company and, in the case of fraud, imprisonment.

Appendices

Appendix 1
Companies Act 1985, Schedule 4

Part 1. Balance Sheet: Format 1

A. CALLED-UP SHARE CAPITAL NOT PAID	May be shown under item C.II.

B. FIXED ASSETS
   I.   INTANGIBLE ASSETS

1. Development costs	
2. Concessions, patents, licences, trade marks and similar rights and assets	May only be included if: (a) the assets were acquired for valuable consideration or (b) the assets were created by the company itself.
3. Goodwill	May only be included if acquired for valuable consideration.
4. Payments on account	

   II.   TANGIBLE ASSETS
       1. Land and buildings
       2. Plant and machinery
       3. Fixtures, fittings, tools and equipment
       4. Payments on account and assets in course of construction.

III. INVESTMENTS
1. Shares in group companies
2. Loans to group companies
3. Shares in related companies
4. Loans to related companies
5. Other investments (other than loans)
6. Other loans
7. Own shares   The nominal value of the shares held shall be shown separately.

C. CURRENT ASSETS
I. STOCKS
1. Raw materials and consumables
2. Work in progress
3. Finished goods and goods for resale
4. Payments on account

II. DEBTORS
1. Trade debtors
2. Amounts owed by group companies
3. Amounts owed by related companies
4. Other debtors
5. Called up share capital, not paid
6. Prepayments and accrued income   May be shown separately at D.

III. INVESTMENTS
1. Shares in group companies
2. Own shares   The nominal value of the shares shall be shown separately.

3. Other investments

IV. CASH AT BANK AND IN HAND

D. PREPAYMENTS AND ACCRUED INCOME

E. CREDITORS: AMOUNTS FALLING DUE WITHIN ONE YEAR

1. Debenture loans	Amounts of any convertible loans shall be shown separately.

2. Bank loans and overdrafts
3. Payments received on account
4. Trade creditors
5. Bills of exchange payable
6. Amounts owed to group companies
7. Amounts owed to related companies

8. Other creditors, including taxation and social security	Taxation and social security shall be shown separately.

9. Accruals and deferred income.

F. NET CURRENT ASSETS (LIABILITIES)

G. TOTAL ASSETS LESS CURRENT LIABILITIES

H. CREDITORS: AMOUNTS FALLING DUE AFTER MORE THAN ONE YEAR

1. Debenture loans	The amount of any convertible loans shall be shown separately.

2. Bank loans and overdrafts
3. Payments received on account
4. Trade creditors
5. Bills of exchange payable
6. Amounts owed to group companies
7. Amounts owed to related companies

8. Other creditors including taxation and social security	Taxation and social security shall be shown separately.

9. Accruals and deferred income.

I. PROVISIONS FOR LIABILITIES AND CHARGES

1. Pensions and similar obligations
2. Taxation, including deferred taxation
3. Other provisions

J. ACCRUALS AND DEFERRED INCOME

> If not shown separately may be shown as indicated in E9 and H9 as appropriate.

K. CAPITAL AND RESERVES
  I.   CALLED UP SHARE CAPITAL

> Allotted share capital and called up capital which has been paid up shall be shown separately.

  II. SHARE PREMIUM ACCOUNT
  III. REVALUATION RESERVE
  IV. OTHER RESERVES
       1. Capital redemption reserve
       2. Reserve for own shares
       3. Reserves provided for by the Articles of Association
       4. Other reserves
  V.   PROFIT AND LOSS ACCOUNT

Part 2. Definition of some items frequently encountered

Subsidiary company

A company owned as to more than 50 per cent of the voting shares by another company.

A wholly owned subsidiary is therefore 100 per cent controlled. In the case of a subsidiary company not wholly owned, there will be a 'minority interest' on consolidation. This item, shown as a liability, is deemed to represent the claims of the minority shareholders on the net assets of the consolidated subsidiary.

Associated company

This is defined as a company, not being a subsidiary company, where, in essence, the ownership of shares is such as to permit 'significant influence' over the affairs of that company. There will be a presumption that this is the case when 20 percent or more of the voting shares are held by the other company.

Accounting treats such investment on an 'equity' basis; that is to say, brings into profit and loss account the appropriate share of profits, whether distributed or not, and increases the cost of the investment by the appropriate proportion of earnings retained in the associated company subsequent to acquisition of the investment.

Capital redemption reserve
The amount transferred from distributable profits to a 'capital redemption reserve' in respect of the redemption or purchase of a company's own shares.

The purpose of the transfer is to avoid diminution in the company's fixed capital.

The reserve must be treated as if it were paid-up capital, but may be used for the issue to members of bonus shares in the company.

Purchase by a company of its own shares
The Companies Act 1985 now permits a company to purchase its own shares – but not wholly to eliminate them. Any shares so purchased have to be cancelled and the directors' report must record the consideration paid and the reasons for the purchase.

The purchase can be effected from one of two sources: either from company resources, in which case there must be a transfer from free reserves to a capital redemption reserve, or from the issue of new shares. In the latter case, a transfer to reserve must take place to cover the shortfall if the proceeds of the new issue are insufficient to purchase the shares.

Deferred taxation
This item, usually but not necessarily a liability, represents the taxation consequence arising from the difference in taxation treatment from the company accounting treatment. These differences arise principally from the incidence of timing between the two treatments. A significant element used to arise in connection with 100 percent taxation capital allowance on the acquisition of an asset, whereas depreciation in the accounts will normally be spread over a number of years. To take the whole taxation benefit in the year of acquisition depresses the charge to taxation and therefore distorts the after-tax results. This distortion will be adjusted by charging tax on the difference between the capital allowance and the accounting depreciation charge and crediting that amount to a deferred taxation account. Part of the credit will be transferred annually to the taxation charge with the intention of achieving conformity between the tax and accounting treatments.

159

Prior year adjustments
These are defined as those material adjustments applicable to prior years which arise from changes in accounting policies and from the correction of fundamental errors. The correct treatment for such items is to restate the corresponding amount for prior years and adjusting the opening balance of retained profits for the year under review.

Statement of Source and Application of Funds

For the (period) ended — 19XX

	£
Source of Funds	
Profit on ordinary activities before tax	750,000
Adjustment for items not involving the movement of funds	
– depreciation	40,000
– goodwill	10,000
– profit on sale of tangible fixed assets	5,000
Funds generated from operations	805,000
Other sources:	
– sales of tangible assets	20,000
– term loan from XYZ Bank	75,000
Total funds generated	900,000
Application of Funds	
– purchase of fixed tangible assets	25,000
– repayment of medium-term loan	300,000
– dividend paid	120,000
– taxation paid	130,000
	575,000
Increase in Working Capital	325,000
Total funds applied	900,000
Movements in Working Capital	
– increase in stock and work in progress	250,000
– increase in debtors	200,000
– (increase) in creditors	(100,000)
Movement in Net Liquid Funds	350,000
– (decrease) in bank balances	(25,000)
Net Increase in Working Capital	325,000

Appendix 3
A Business Plan Framework

1. **Business mission**
   A statement of the business which the company perceives itself to be in and its intentions in that chosen field.

2. **Background**
   A statement of recent history and current involvement.

3. **Corporate objectives**
   - business development and growth
   - financial
   - quality criteria
   - employee participation and motivation
   - communications
   - exit

4. **Marketing plan**
   - market research and analysis
     - market size, composition and trends
     - competition
     - market share and position
     - future market development
   - market strategy
   - product positioning
   - pricing policies and margins
   - servicing policy
   - advertising and promotion
   - design
   - communications

5. **Product plan**
   - identification of opportunities
   - protection
   - product innovation and development

6. **Sales plan**
    - order intake and backlog
    - margins
    - price and discount policy
    - introductory offers
    - sales force
    - remuneration
    - advertising, promotion and PR
    - communication
    - after-sales service

7. **Operations plan**
    - product development
    - product sourcing
    - quality criteria
    - product, operating and unit costs
    - operating standards
    - research

8. **Manpower plan**
    - planned requirements
      - categories
      - qualities
      - skills
    - selection and recruitment
    - training and development
    - industrial relations and communications
    - pay and benefits

9. **Technical plan**
    - technical intelligence
    - developing technical solutions
    - system specifications
    - space requirements
    - initiate technical proposals

10. **Organisation and control plan**
    - projection of requirements
    - organisation plan
    - communications

11. **Financial plan**
    - profit and loss accounts
    - balance sheets
    - cash flows
    - funding requirements and plans
      - short
      - medium
      - long
    - reports

12. **Communications plan**
    - external
      - trading
      - customers
      - intelligence
      - markets
    - internal
      - operational
      - philosophy
      - financial
      - control
    - design
    - audio and visual aids
    - electronic communications

13. **Risk analysis and contingency plan**
    - order intake
    - margins
    - fixed costs
    - liquidity

14. **Action plan**

Appendix 4
The Business Expansion Scheme

Summary of the principal legislative provisions relating to the Business Expansion Scheme.

1. **Introduction**
   The scheme was introduced by Section 26 of the Finance Act 1983. There have been a number of amendments in subsequent legislation. The rules governing taxation relief do not therefore necessarily apply consistently throughout the period since 1983. The summary below represents the situation subsequent to the Finance Act 1987, but the legislation is complex and professional advice should be obtained in specific cases.

2. **Tax relief**
   Tax relief is given against income tax effectively at the claimant's highest rate of tax in the year in which shares are issued subject to the following conditions:

   - The claimant must be a qualifying individual who subscribes for new eligible shares, ie ordinary shares which carry no preferential rights.
   - The company must be a qualifying unquoted company.
   - The shares must have been used for the purpose of raising money for a qualifying trade.
   - The shares subscribed for must be for bona fide commercial purposes and not as part of a scheme or arrangement the main purpose, or one of the main purposes of which, is the avoidance of tax.
   - The trade is being, or will within two years be, carried on by the company or a qualifying subsidiary.

167

- The claim may be made when the trade has been carried on for not less four months and must be made within two years after the end of the year of assessment, (ie in which the shares are issued) to which the claim relates.
- The Finance Act 1987 permits an investor to claim up to half of the amount subscribed for shares issued between 6 April and 5 October in any tax year, commencing in 1987-88, as a deduction from his total income for the previous tax year, subject to a maximum of £5,000.
- The maximum amount eligible for relief is £40,000 in any one tax year and, for direct investment, may not be less than £500 in any one company in any tax year.
- Relief is withdrawn if the conditions cease to be satisfied within three years of the making of the investment or if the shares are disposed of within five years.
- Relief is wholly or partly withdrawn if the claimant receives value from the company. Value is received if, for example, the company redeems the shares or makes a loan to the claimant.

3. **Capital Gains Tax**
   Where shares are disposed of and relief has not been withdrawn, any gain arising will not be a chargeable gain (nor will any loss be allowable).

4. **Qualifying companies**
   The requirements for a company to qualify under this scheme are:
   - incorporated and resident only in the UK
   - not quoted on the Stock Exchange or dealt with on the Unlisted Securities Market
   - not a subsidiary of, or controlled by, any other companay
   - all its share capital is fully paid
   - it must carry on a qualifying trade (or exist to hold shares in qualifying subsidiaries)
   - it may have subsidiaries if, throughout the relevant period, those subsidiaries are at least 90 per cent owned and exist to carry on a qualifying trade, or are property managing or dormant
   - a company will not qualify if the value of its land and buildings (after deducting certain liabilities) exceeds one-half of the net value of the company's net assets
   - a company will not qualify if the value of its trade is mainly carried on outside the UK.

5. Qualifying trades

A company carrying on any trade for bona fide commercial purposes with a view to profit will qualify, subject to the following exclusions:

- dealing in commodities, shares, securities or futures
- dealing in goods otherwise than in the course of ordinary trade of wholesale or retail distribution.
- banking, insurance, money lending, debt factoring, hire purchase financing or other financial activities
- oil extraction
- leasing or receiving royalties or licence fees
- providing legal or accountancy services
- farming
- property development, if the company has an interest in the land.

Special rules apply in the following cases:
- film production
- research and development activities
- oil exploration
- ship chartering.

Principal Differences Between a Public and a Private Company

		Public (plc)	**Private**
1.	**Raising money**		May not offer shares or debentures to the public.
2.	**Rights issues** Section 89 gives a statutory right of pre-emption to ordinary shareholders in the case of a new issue of shares for cash.	The rights may be disapplied either by a provision in the Articles or by special resolution within five years. (Stock Exchange rules one year.)	The rights may be disapplied without time limit in the Memorandum or Articles or within a time limt as per plc rules.
3.	**Allotment of shares**	(a) May not allot shares unless at least 25 per cent of the nominal value and the whole of any premium has been paid. (b) May not allot shares in consideration for an undertaking to do work or perform services for the company.	

	Public (plc)	**Private**
	(c) If shares are allotted for a non-cash consideration, the contract must be performed within five years.	
4. Maintenance of share capital	If net assets fall below 50 per cent of called up share capital, an extra-ordinary general meeting must be called within 28 days of awareness of the situation.	
5. Distributions	In addition to the provisions under Section 263 applicable to all companies, there is a capital rule under Section 264 which provides that distributions may only be made provided the net assets (before and after the distribution) are not less than the aggregate of the called-up share capital and its undistributable reserves.	Section 263 applies. There is no capital maintenance rule.

		Public (plc)	Private
6.	Directors' loans	No company may make loans to directors, or give guarantees in connection with such loans under Sections 330-331. In addition, in the case of a public company, quasi-loans under section 331 are prohibited to directors and persons connected with directors.	
7.	Purchase of own shares	Companies may now purchase their own shares subject to rigorous rules set out in the Companies Act. In general, these are that the purchase must be made from distributable profits or the proceeds of a fresh issue.	May purchase own shares out of capital subject to the provisions of Section 171 *et seq*.
8.	Financial assistance for acquisition of shares	Prohibited from giving financial assistance except in accordance with the detailed provisions in Chapter VI, Companies Act 1985.	May provide financial assistance in connection with the purchase of shares in a private company subject to the provisions of Section 155.

		Public (plc)	**Private**
9.	Reporting	Must lay accounts before the members within seven months of the end of the accounting reference period.	May take advantage of the special provision relating to 'small' and 'medium' sized companies and may extend the reporting period to 10 months.
10.	Directors	Minimum of two directors. May not appoint a person to be a director over age 70 at the time. However, the Articles may vary this requirement, as can an ordinary resolution of which special notice of 28 days has been given.	A sole director may act.
11.	Company secretary	Must be professionally qualified.	
12.	Off market purchases (Section 164)	There must be a specific contract and a special resolution, which must determine a date on which the authority will expire, being not later than 18 months after the date of the resolution.	Does not require a specific termination date.

Appendix 6
Public Offerings

Part 1

Outline of Contents of Listing Particulars required by Section 142 of the Financial Services Act 1986

1. Details concerning the issuer, including the names of the directors and a declaration that they accept responsibility for the information contained in the listing particulars.
2. In the case of a statement or report attributed to an expert, a statement that he has given (and not withdrawn) his consent to the issue of the listing particulars.
3. Names and addresses of the auditors, the issuer's bankers, solicitors and sponsoring brokers.
4. A statement that application will be made to the Council of the Stock Exchange for the securities to be admitted to the official list.
5. Details concerning the securities for which application is made, including the nature and amount of the issue, the number of securities to be created, a description of the shares and of the rights attaching to them, their transferability, and the registrars. The issue or offer price, and pre-emption rights.
6. Summary of the provisions of the issuer's Memorandum and Articles of Association.
7. Underwriting arrangements, proceeds of the issue, fees payable to financial intermediaries. Purposes to which the proceeds of the issue will be applied.
8. Statement by the directors that the working capital is sufficient or, if not, how the additional working capital will be satisfied.
9. Details of the share offerings within the current and preceding financial year, take-over offers and the prices at which such transactions have taken place. Details of arrangements, if the listing relates to a rights or capitalisation issue.

175

10. General information about the issue and its capital including:
    - if 10 percent or more of the voting capital is unissued a statement that no material issue of shares will take place within one year without shareholders' approval.
    - convertible debt and conversion terms
    - summary of the operations affecting the issued capital of the company during the three preceding years and the terms therof
    - indication of the persons able jointly or severally to exercise control over the issuer
    - names of any persons (other than a director) who is interested, directly or indirectly, in 5 per cent or more of the issuer's capital, and details thereof
    - details of any of the shares owned by the issuer
    - details concerning share options
    - information concerning any legal or similar proceedings within the preceding 12 months which may have significant effect on the financial position
    - details of material contracts (other than in the ordinary course of business) entered into within the preceding two years.
    - place where specified documents may be inspected.
11. Details about the issuer's principal business activities, its products, turnover by category and geographical market during the previous three years, places of business, dependence on intellectual property rights, research and development policy, employee numbers and investments in other undertakings.
12. Financial information concerning the issuer:
    - profits and losses, assets and liabilities and financial record in the form of an accountant's report (as specified) for each of the last five completed financial years, together with a comparative table
    - statement that the annual accounts have been audited (and any qualification in the reports)
    - profit or loss per share arising out of the issuer's ordinary activities, after tax, for each of the last three financial years (adjusted, if necessary, to a comparable basis)
    - dividends per share for each of the last three financial years
    - if more than nine months have elapsed since the end of the financial year to which the last published annual accounts relate, an interim financial statement covering at least the first six months of the current financial year
    - statement of any significant change in the financial or trading

position which has occurred since the end of the last financial year or the last interim financial statement

- the source and application of funds over each of the past three financial years
- details, as specified, of interests in other undertakings held for the long term and likely to have a significant effect on the assessment of the financial position and also in those cases where the issuer holds at least 10 per cent of the capital
- details of loan capital, borrowings, mortgages and charges (identifying guaranteed and secured borrowings and debts) and the total amount of any contingent liabilities or guarantees at the most recent practicable date.

13. Details concerning the directors and their remuneration and other benefits, service contracts, and unusual significant transactions.

Their interests relating to the securities to be listed as specified in the Companies Act 1985, loans to or guarantees in favour of directors.

14. Details of any schemes involving the employees in the share capital.

15. A summary of the specified powers relating to directors in the Articles of Association.

Part 2

Outline of the statutory information relating to a prospectus required by Part I, Schedule 3 Companies Act 1985

1. The number of founders or management or deferred shares (if any) and the nature and extent of the interest of the holders in the property and profits of the company.

2. The directors' share qualification (if any) and any provision in the Articles as to their remuneration.

3. The names, descriptions and addresses of directors and proposed directors.

4. Particulars of the 'minimum subscription'.

This is the amount of money required to provide for:

- the purchase price of any property to be defrayed wholly or partly out of the proceeds of the issue
- the preliminary expenses and commission payable to persons who have agreed to subscribe or obtain subscriptions for shares

- the repayment of any monies borrowed by the company in respect of the foregoing
- working capital

The prospectus must state the amounts to be provided for any of these items otherwise than out of the proceeds of the issue and the sources from which they are to be provided.

5. The time of the opening of the subscription lists.

6. The amount payable on application and allotment on each share including the amount, if any, payable by way of premium; and details of shares offered and allotted for cash within the previous two years and the amount paid on the shares allotted including the amount, if any, paid by way of premium.

7. Where the company has given to a person or persons an option to subscribe for the company's shares or debentures, the prospectus must state who such persons are and the sum they will have to pay for the shares subject to the options, what consideration they gave for the option and for how long it is exercisable.

8. Details of shares and debentures issued in the two preceding years for a consideration other than cash, with particulars of the consideration given.

9. Where the company proposes to use the proceeds of the issue wholly or partly to pay for property which it has acquired or proposes to acquire (other than in the normal course of business unconnected with the issue), then the prospectus must state the names and addresses of the vendors and the total purchase price, distinguishing cash, shares or debentures.

10. Where a business is being purchased with the proceeds of the issue, the amount being paid for goodwill must be shown separately.

11. Underwriting commissions.

12. The amount of preliminary expenses and the expenses of the issue.

13. Any amount or benefit paid or given within the two preceding years or intended to be paid or given to any promoter, and the consideration he gave for such payment or benefit.

14. The dates and parties to, and the general nature of, any material contract entered into within two years prior to the issue of the prospectus, not being a contract entered into in the ordinary course of business carried on or intended to be carried on by the company.

15. The names and addresses of the auditors of the company.

16. The interest of each director (or any firm of which the director is a member) in the promotion of the company or the property to be acquired by it.

17. The rights attaching to the various classes of shares which form the company's capital.
18. The length of time for which the company's business or the business (if any) to be acquired by the company has been carried on if less than three years.

Outline of reports required by Part II of Schedule 3

1. • A report by the company's auditors on the financial position of the company and its subsidiaries, if any (either grouped or otherwise), in respect of the profit and loss accounts of each of the five financial years immediately preceding the prospectus and the balance sheet at that date.
   • The rates of dividend (if any) paid by the company in respect of each class of shares in respect of each of the immediately preceding five financial years.
   • If no accounts have been made up in respect of any part of the five years ending on a date three months before the issue of the prospectus, the report shall contain a statement of that fact.
2. A report by the accountant named in the prospectus regarding the financial position of any business to be acquired (or the shares in any company which will become a subsidiary company), covering in respect of the profit and losses of each of the five financial years (or such lesser number of years as the case may be) immediately preceding the issue of the prospectus and a balance sheet at the latest accounting date; and in respect of any subsidiary company to be acquired the amount which would have been distributable to the members of the holding company and the minority interests.
3. If any adjustments are made to the figures covered in either of these reports, the reports shall indicate what those adjustments are.

Outline Heads of a Placing Document

Details of shares placed
    Share capital
    Indebtedness

Glossary

Key information
    Summary
    Trading record (five years)
    Placing statistics

Directors and advisers

Introduction

History

Industry background

Business
    Summary
    Areas of business
    Customers and markets
    Marketing and sales
    Competition
    Research and development
    Premises

Management
 Board
 Managing director(s)
 Executive directors
 Management
 Employees
 Pension scheme
 Share ownership for employees

Financial information
 Summary
 Price-earnings ratio
 Dividends
 Net tangible assets

Reasons for the placing

Prospects

Accountants' reports
 Introduction
 Accounting policies
 Consolidated profit and loss accounts
 Consolidated source and application
 of funds statement
 Consolidated balance sheets

Additional information
 Incorporation and share capital
 Group structure
 Memorandum and Articles of Association
 Share option schemes
 Directors and other interests
 Property holdings
 Placing Arrangements
 Material contracts
 Employee participation
 Commercial contracts
 Research and development expenditure
 Taxation
 General
 Documents available for inspection

Appendix 8
Timetable for Achieving a Stock Exchange Listing

Note D = decision day (or impact day)

Serial	Event	Timing completion date	Remarks
1.	Select issuing house	D-26W	Discussions with two or three potential houses
2.	Select broker	D-26W	Advice from issuing house and discussions with two or three potential brokers
3.	Select PR agency	D-26W	Discussions with two or three firms invited to tender. Note: Consideration must be given to other corporate advertising and promotion work which may be co-ordinated with the offering publicity.

183

Serial	Event	Timing completion date	Remarks
4.	Draft long form report available from reporting accountants	D-17W	May or may not be company auditors
5.	Submit draft Articles of Association to Stock Exchange	D-16W	
6.	Projected year end results available	D-15W	This assumes offer will take place around three months after year end
7.	Decision to proceed		
8.	Outline draft prospectus available	D-13W	
9.	Company financial year end	D-13W	
10.	Appoint receiving bankers, registrars and printers	D-10W	
11.	Circulate first draft prospectus	D-9W	
12.	Decision on method of flotation	D-9W	
13.	First draft of offer for sale agreement	D-8W	

Serial	Event	Timing completion date	Remarks
14.	Commence preparation of advertising material and other printed work	D-8W	
15.	Company formally resolves all matters necessary for public offering status	D-6W	
16.	Final draft of short form report. Long form report in final form. Approve annual report and accounts	D-4W	
		In days	
17.	Commence publicity	D-30	
18.	All clearances to have been received from Stock Exchange	D-17	
19.	Dividend forecast. Indebtedness report	D-10	
20.	Final circulation of proof documents	D-7	
21.	First issue pricing meeting	D-6	
22.	Final checking of all documentation	D-3	

Serial	Event	Timing completion date	Remarks
23.	Provisional issue price fixed. Employee announcement re issue	D-2	
24.	Final proofs of prospectus and advertisements	D-1	
25.	Issue price decision	D-1	
26.	Stock Exchange approves all documents. Company board approves all documents. Offer for sale agreement signed	D-1	
27.	Announce public offering. Underwriting completed. All documents to Stock Exchange. Press conference	D day	
28.	Prospectus advertised in at least two national newspapers	D+3	
29.	Listing granted by Stock Exchange	D+6	
30.	Receiving bank closes lists	D+7	
31.	Shares allotted	D+13	
32.	Dealings commence	D+14	

Further Reading from Kogan Page

Be Your Own Company Secretary, AJ Scrine, 1987
Debt Collection Made Easy, P Buckland, 1987
Finance and Accounts for Managers, Desmond Goch, 1986
Financial Management for the Small Business: a Daily Telegraph Guide, 2nd edn, Colin Barrow, 1988
Going for Growth: A Guide to Corporate Strategy, Michael K Lawson, 1987
A Handbook of Management Techniques, Michael Armstrong, 1986
How to Be an Even Better Manager, Michael Armstrong, 1988
How to Deal with Your Bank Manager, Geoffrey Sales, 1988
How to Make Meetings Work, Malcolm Peel, 1988
Law for the Small Business: a Daily Telegraph Guide, 5th edition, Patricia Clayton, 1987
Management Accountancy for the Company Executive, TM Walker, 1987
Never Take No for an Answer, Samfrits le Poole, 1987
A Practical Guide to Creative Accounting, Michael Jameson, 1988
The Practice of Successful Business Management, Kenneth Winckles, 1986
Profits from Improved Productivity, Fiona Halse and John Humphrey, 1988
Raising Finance: the Guardian Guide for the Small Business, 3rd edition, Clive Woodcock, 1988
Successful Expansion for the Small Business: a Daily Telegraph Guide, MJ Morris, 1984
Takeovers, Acquisitions and Mergers, EA Stallworthy and OM Kharbanda, 1988

Index